The Magic
of
CRAZYTIVITY

-7 Magician's Secrets to Unleash Your Creativity,
Trigger Innovation and Change Your Life -

The Magic of Crazytivity

7 Magician's Secrets to Unleash Your Creativity,
Trigger Innovation and Change Your Life

By Butzi

ISBN-13: 978-1791931223

Independently published

First edition 2019

Design and layout by Atelier Mayanne Trias

Cover by Sami Zran photographer and Atelier Mayanne Trias.

Printed with Createspace.

To Diana,

Secret #2 Reclaim Your Childhood Superpowers

Secret #3 Overcome Your ▮ Obstacles and Fear

Secret #4 Use Crazytivity 81

103 Secret #5 Connect the Dots ▬

Secret #6 Change Your Habits to Cultivate Your Creativity

139 Secret #7 – Dare to Create for the Real World

Foreword by Sonia Choquette

How easily we forget that creativity is an innate magical power. As children, we had it, and never gave it a second thought. But then, as time went by we were taught that creative fun is for recess, and we need to move on to more serious matters…and then recess went away. For far too many of us, as we grew up, the creative spark got dimmer and dimmer.

The good news is that we all still possess this creative spark. Even if it has dimmed a bit, with a little assistance, we can turn it up right now. In my opinion, we must. Creativity is our greatest super power. It is what makes our lives happen. We need it in order to be happy. Successful. Abundant Healthy. We cannot afford to let the spark go out.

If we do, we lose our power, our potential, and quite frankly lose our capacity for joy. Life without our creativity on hand becomes dull, depressing, and boring.

Besides, when you reawaken your creativity, you simultaneously reawaken another great and innate super power–your intuition. That is because they are two ends of the same spectrum and go together. With creativity and intuition running your show in life, the sky is the limit. Without them, the light is out, and you cannot see the sky at all.

Fortunately for all of us, once in a while, some magical person comes along who truly understands this. Someone who didn't lose their spark of creativity, someone whose intuition is up and running beautifully, and whose magic and mojo are alive and well. Such a magician engages us in such interesting, fun, surprising, and unexpected ways so that our creativity and intuition spontaneously re-awaken, and once again, we feel our own innate magic come alive.

Meeting Butzi at a dinner party in Paris, I instantly knew he was such a one. Before we even sat down to the meal, he had all the dinner guests laughing so hard and was so much fun that the evening was pure joy. Fueled by Butzi's creative spark, our genius ideas were unleashed, and during the evening they just kept getting brighter and more brilliant by the hour. By the end of the night we all went home feeling like superstars.

The second time Butzi and I met was at yet another dinner party where he mesmerized us guests with his magic tricks. Looking around at our faces, I could tell each of us came alive with awe and wonder as he made the impossible possible. As we watched him perform his magic, we somehow felt a bit of our own. After he finished his show, our conversations began to take off again– becoming more interesting, engaging, and yes, really creative. We all wanted to be magicians too, and with Butzi's boost, that evening we were. That is "The Butzi Effect."

In The Magic of Crazitivity, Butzi will ignite this kind of creative magic in you. In it, he offers quick and effective tools that re-awaken your creativity and get it flowing quickly. I've tried them. They work. They are fun. They are easy. They pack a punch. And they get life flowing.

Best yet, his tools move you quickly past any resistance or doubt you may have about your own creative genius and on to seeing just how fabulously creative you really are.
So, take this book and run with it. Go on. Don't settle for being stuck, bored, and uninspired. Don't live without the creative spark inside of you shining brightly. Embrace Butzi's "nothing is impossible" outlook, and unleash your own crazy creativity now. It will brighten your life and help you become magical in every way.

Sonia Choquette

New York Times best-selling author of
Your Three Best Super Powers

Introduction

What if I told you that you could create a more meaningful and exciting life, full of possibilities? A life in which you can break out of boring routines while having more impact on your company, your family, your friends, and even the world? A life full of purpose in which you feel more alive than ever? I bet you would be very interested—but maybe a bit skeptical. Most of us have tried for excellence and failed—and it's discouraging when obstacles come in the way of exciting projects and successes. It's especially frustrating when we don't know how to overcome our creative weaknesses or how to make use of our imagination to solve problems, form lasting solutions, and create excitement in the everyday. That is why I wrote this book: to teach you how you can create new ideas, projects, and think outside the box to find original ideas and solutions to situations you are stuck in.

But how do we become creative? Is creativity a gift that is only meant for certain people? No. Definitely not. It is for you, me, and all other human beings on the planet. In this book, you will discover how we all have hidden creative capacities that can be activated, developed, and nurtured to become super inventive and achieve what we want.

I talk from experience as I managed to live from my passion for 10 years: magic. I even created dozens of illusions for various companies and colleagues and have written two books. I wouldn't have believed those things possible if I'd heard them 10 years ago. Luckily, I was fortunate to be crazy enough to try. I discovered later that it is exactly how successful magicians do their best work—we create what is said to be impossible. We impress our audiences by creatively working through improbable situations, and that is what I practiced in the last decade. Now, the good news is that we are not superhumans and you don't need to be a magician to learn what it takes to think like we do and create the success you want to have! For that, you need to incorporate…

The hidden power of the crazytivity mindset

Let me ask you this: what do you think the difference in creativity is between two different, knowledgeable people? It isn't what they know but what they do with what they know. This is exactly what creativity is about—cooking with the same ingredients but creating different, original recipes. And to do this, you need a specific approach, a powerful mindset, and simple tools that creative people master, consciously or not. I like to rename this mindset *Crazytivity*.

For those who didn't get it, Crazytivity is "crazyness" and "creativity" in one word (I think you got it, but we never know). It is a word I have invented...until I discovered it already existed in some "Urban Dictionary" online. So I guess I just found it by myself. I decided to use it because I truly think that we need a bit of crazyness to take action on the thoughts we have created and I think that it reflects perfectly most magicians and entrepreneurs' mindset. It is about imagining the wildest projects, the ideas that will make you or others happy, and undertaking all that it takes to create the changes you want to see in the world, even -and especially- if you sound crazy. It is about reconnecting with your inner child and giving him the knowledge, the experience, and the freedom of creative power.

Most people underestimate what a powerful mindset can do for them. I would argue, it is almost everything. It gives you a different perspective on what happens around you. Instead of seeing obstacles that come your way as impassable walls, you will see the 1001 solutions and ways to keep going forward by climbing that wall, destroying it, going through it, or bypassing it. Crazytivity will help you become an optimist who sees many opportunities. When others feel like they've reached a dead end, Crazytivity will help you take your dreams and crazy projects seriously.

If you acquire such a mindset, it will be easy to learn creative tools, techniques, methods, and any knowledge you need to achieve your dreams. And the good news? You don't need to be a genius for that. Yes, I can say I'm creative, and I accomplished things that were supposed to be "impossible," but I'm not a genius! I wish it were the case, but I don't understand things more easily than others, I haven't created fantastic inventions, and I'm not super knowledgeable. And you know what? I don't care because my mindset will always allow me to create a solution by playing with my strengths.

For me, it is just a matter of approach and time to achieve what seems unattainable. This is what I accomplished with a Crazytivity mindset. I became a professional magician and made it my job for 10 years. Then I started creating illusions for myself, for my clients, and (something that I thought I was completely incapable of) for my colleagues! Parallel to that, I studied acting for three years and became a professional actor, making appearances on French television. I even wrote, interpreted, directed, and edited a movie with a friend. I gave body and mind creative workshop in various countries around the world and then wrote a book for magicians teaching them to create their own magic. Apart from that, I gave two TEDx talks, performed in London West End and at the prestigious Magic Castle in Hollywood, and have two black belts in martial arts (Judo and Sambo) as well National Championship medals. I've composed two little piano pieces, play ukulele, chess, I surf, and speak four languages.

Again, I don't say this to brag so that you applaud in wonder (although that would be nice, thank you if you did), but to tell you that I'm 100% sure it has to do with my mindset and the creative ideas and approach I put into practice. I observed, analyzed and took classes with people who achieved great things. It turns out that they all have this particular mindset, too! So…

Attention please – this is what is going to happen before your very eyes

In this book, I commit to helping you: find back the natural qualities that you were gifted with, to believe in your creative capacities, and to become crazy enough to reach for the impossible. To do that, I'll first show you what is so special about you and how you can express it. Then. I will teach you how to reconnect with your inner child to unleash the crazy imagination you naturally had as a kid, without the filters you've probably accumulated over the years. After that, we will see how to overcome your fears and obstacles so that you can finally access the Crazytivity mindset. Once you discover how to think creatively, you will learn a powerful brainstorming method so that you have what it takes to achieve what is said to be impossible. And last but not least, we will see how to take action on your ideas and bring your ideas to the real world to concretize them. All those things aren't complicated at all to learn, and I can guarantee you it will be a fun adventure to try those new ways of thinking with me!

What results can you expect?

The power of making your every day exciting, your work fun, and your wildest dreams achievable. The possibility of living the life you have Imagined, chosen, and that you will build, finding solutions to obstacles in front of you. You can become the "solution person" who is never worried about whatever life throws into your way. And just in case you were wondering: yes, you can make more money with creativity. If you see it as a tool to expand your possibilities, know that creativity will help you with that. Doing something differently, using your resources better and finding original ideas to answer common problems can certainly generate revenue. Whether you find great ideas for your own business with new projects (which lead to new goals, a new purpose, or hundreds of solutions to everyday problems), or you increase your value inside your company (mental agility and entrepreneurial qualities have never been more valuable), it sets you apart from others who don't think by themselves.

Creativity will settle in all the layers of your everyday job—it can help you find new and effective ways to communicate with colleagues who have strong personalities, organize your workday better, thus gaining time and be more productive, and manage your team more efficiently. We are all searching for ways to live a meaningful life, and this will help you discover what drives you, how you can best make a difference, and do something about it.

Are you ready for that?! So…

…Let's dive into this crazytivity adventure!

Secret #1
We Are All Magic

Magician's Reveal

This might shock you, but I don't believe in magic. Like many of my peers, I don't believe a person can really bend a spoon with his mind. I can do it because I know the trick; I know the sleight of hand that gives the illusion of it. But I don't believe that anyone can levitate while meditating, and I don't believe anyone can hold his hand above a flame then make the 3rd degree burn instantly disappear.

These are illusions; they are physical and psychological tricks. And don't get me wrong, we magicians want to believe these illusions; the problem is: no one can actually prove they can really do it. There is even a one-million-dollar prize for anyone who can prove they have such superpowers (check it out, I'm not kidding!)

However, this doesn't mean I don't believe in another kind of magic. I do believe that human beings have magical powers such as the power to communicate without talking, the power to inspire each other, and the power to create. Human beings have the magical ability of making new thoughts appear. This magic is invisible but right here; it surrounds us like water surrounds a fish. Creativity is a magical power that is innate. We have the gift to generate ideas; we can produce original visions from nothing. We can transform preexisting concepts and make them new.

My skeptical magician brain still tells me, "There must be a scientific explanation to that!"

Even if I hear someone say, "Neuronal connections create a vibration in the brain that generates blah blah blah ..." or "Throughout evolution, it is easy to understand that the human brain's chemistry changed so that blah blah blah ..."— I just hear "MAGIC."

No one can say where the first form of intelligence originated or explain how we became gifted with such powers. When I can't explain it, I just accept it. I let the magic be.

In this book, and in this chapter especially, I will describe what kind of magic we were naturally gifted with and how we can use it to create more magic. You will then be allowed to do your own research on how and why. But first, let me show you how magical you are. Are you ready? Let's go!

Creativity is in Your Blood

Creativity is one reason humans have survived and evolved throughout thousands and thousands of years. We are not the only species with this ability. Creativity is everywhere in nature. It protects animals and plants through camouflage. It helps them defend and nourish themselves in a thousand different ways ... humans too! Creativity is in our DNA. The more we evolved, the more we wanted to thrive and develop. Therefore, the more discoveries we made the better we became at being inventive and creative. We, humans, have developed this skill to another level, and that is precisely why we evolved into who we are today! This is why when we create something, whether it is a solution, an idea, or a new way of doing things, it feels good.

So, it is not about knowing if you are creative or not. You are creative; this is CERTAIN.

This fact is historically researched and scientifically proven: Creativity runs through your blood. What you may not have is the feeling of being creative. You may not know how to "do it." You may feel that you are just using ideas that have already been created by others. You may feel like you're not an original, that you are not a "creative genius." If this is what you are feeling, don't worry. This book is about identifying and enhancing that feeling, step by step, until you understand these doubts are all smoke and mirrors hiding your true capabilities. Top innovators, artists, and creators all acknowledge that, even when they don't feel creative, they know deep down they are capable of creativity. They know that nature has gifted them with a free superpower. YOU are gifted with this superpower. Creativity, ingenuity, and originality are all within you, in one form or another. Now, you have the task of adopting small habits and attitudes every day to help these gifts flow out of you. Although this natural creativity might come out of you differently than it does from your colleagues or friends — it doesn't matter! We are all different, and that is why creativity is an unlimited and unique skill for anyone.

Don't hold back your uniqueness and imagination—the world needs it! So, do it: acknowledge it out loud! Let's be crazy and say this out loud: "Whether I want it or not, I am creative." If you are in the subway, share this declaration with your neighbor. Okay, you can whisper it quietly to yourself —but do it ! Even in the worst-case scenario, it will still be fun.

Meet Your Inner Genie

"Say, you're a lot smaller than my last master. Either that, or I'm getting bigger. Look at me from the side. Do I look different to you?"

- The Genie, Aladdin -

What problem do we often have? We don't know how to open the door to our creativity. You might not know where to start, or maybe you haven't felt creative in a while. However, not feeling creative doesn't reflect anything about your IDENTITY. It doesn't mean you aren't creative, it just means you think that you aren't. And if you believe that you aren't creative, you won't accomplish anything. If you believe in your abilities, you will open your eyes to every creative opportunity that surrounds you. You will try and you will learn; you will finally create something. No other skills are required to become a great creator. The greatest artists throughout history weren't just « lucky », they trusted their inner genie and actively looked more for clues, connections and inspiration to generate great ideas ! It's all a matter of perspective and mindset.

The first thing I'd like for you to recognize is the genie you have inside of you. I know you can't really see him, but trust me, he's there. Actually, he is bored because you overlook him all the time. If you acknowledge him, and even trust him, you will magically create connections. You will begin to see things others don't. You will create original ideas and solutions, and will gain confidence in your creative skills. This confidence will help you generate better ideas and better solutions for your problems. It will help you live an extraordinary, passionate life.

If you ignore your inner genie, you can be sure to never experience creativity. The solutions you find won't be original. You will sit in front of empty white pages with no ideas other than what's been done before. You won't know how to be remarkable, how to shine your uniqueness. One thing may lead to another, and you could end up sleeping under a bridge, begging for pocket change for beer. Is that what you want for your life?! Okay, maybe I exaggerated the last bit— but you get my point.

So, what can you do now? Make a commitment to yourself. Buy a journal and write down this commitment. You are committing to train your already existing creativity; you're making the decision to take care of your inner genie. You are deciding to thrive and shine in this world through the magic you were gifted with! This is the first step; this is the moment where you shift something in your brain.

The Stupid Story of How I Started Trusting My Inner Genie

As my German aunt's 60th birthday approached, we decided to do something "special." I was already doing magic and had even started to make money with it. When my mother asked if I would perform in front of everyone, I was happy to oblige. But what could the rest of the family do for my aunt?

My mother came up with a couple of different ideas; she listed things my aunt liked and had done in her life. She thought of creating a slide show, but she knew this would be such an obvious gift that wouldn't be that fun. She asked me for other ideas. For some reason, I was creative in my mother's eyes. I really hadn't created anything substantial just yet, but she knew me.

She came to me and said, " Butzi, you are creative. Can you help us find a good idea? "

I immediately felt inspired. I don't know where it came from, but I said, " We should do something funnier, something crazier than a slide-show."

We had a real stage, and I thought it would be a waste to not use it for some kind of mise-en-scène. I suggested, " Why not do something crazy on that stage? "

That was the starting point. We began brainstorming what to do:

- Me: "Let's see… what does she like?"
- Mom: "She likes fashion, classical music, sewing, clothes and making costumes, children, and classical dance, especially the ballet Swan Lake."

[Pause here: do you see all of the starting point opportunities for new ideas?]

-Me: "Ok, we could do something with dancing maybe, since we have a stage?"

-Mom: "Yes, but we aren't exactly good enough at dancing to be giving a show."

-Me: "What if we exaggerate it and make it funny? Why not dress up as a ballerina and dance for her?"

-Mom: "Okay...but who would do it?"

-Me: "I could do it, but it would be funnier if we were all there... Dad, Ben (my brother in law), and I. "

So, we stuck with this plan and ended up with a HUGE hit. We were three hairy men dressed as classical ballerinas; we actually learned exaggerated choreography of Swan Lake to make my aunt laugh. When I think back now, I realize something: Not only did we create an idea, we created a meaningful gift— a hilarious and unique moment, a special memory for my family to always keep. We put effort into it, and although she was crying of laughter, I'm sure she was smiling in gratitude as well. After this moment, I got hooked on creativity. I began to put much more effort and confidence into my projects; I began to trust my inner genie more and more.

You can do this too. You don't need my mother to ask you to do so. I'm telling you now, you are creative. I'd like you to shine your creativity on the very next opportunity that arises.

Your Magical Moments

Let me ask you this question: where and when do have your best ideas? Chances are, your response was something like: in the shower, when you're going for a walk, while driving, when you are falling asleep, or when you're half asleep.

I once asked this question in a conference and someone responded with, "When I'm drunk."

Another response was, "When I'm in the toilet."

Why not? My point is, everyone has those moments of inspiration. I'm pretty sure you didn't answer with, "I don't have them." This is just another clue that you are already creative.

These moments of inspiration are beautiful. We feel like there is no limit to what we can do, that we have finally found the solution to our problems. I decided to call those moments "magical moments," as we have no idea where they come from or how it is even possible to have them. We could explain them through psychology and science, but even with such an explanation, it would still look and feel like magic to most of us. These moments make us feel like our inner genie is on fire!

Now, I have another question: What do you do in these moments?

If you don't know what I mean, I'm pretty sure you are not taking these moments seriously. Any creator who trusts their inner genie will capture them moments; they'll write down their ideas in order to make these concrete later. That is the main difference between creative people and those who block their creativity it is not the quality of their ideas that varies, but the fact that creative people take their ideas seriously. Magicians always take each new idea seriously, even (and especially!) if the idea is stupid, impossible, or absurd. We won't let them disappear in a puff of smoke or dematerialize from our mind. You may think, *Oh, I'll remember this idea later*…and then poof! Gone. As magicians, we envision, and we must trust those moments. The more you trust these creative moments, the more they will come.

The first step in discovering your inner genie, and in reconnecting with your natural creativity, is to acknowledge it the very moment it comes to you. I'm not talking about actively searching for ideas (we will get to that later). I'm talking about taking care of the ideas that come to you. Take care of them, write them down and nurture them. Later, come back to them and you will slowly discover how much of a genius you really are.

So, Where Should You Start?

"Start where you are. Use what you have. Do what you can."
- Arthur Ashe -

Amazing artists and creators often sound mysterious when they discuss their creative process. They say things like, "Well, I just do it ... I feel in the zone and I just write a song."
Great! Thank you, Hendrix. After years of study and experimentation, I know about this "zone" we may hear about. However, when I was just starting out and craving to be more creative, hearing other artists discuss the process wasn't helpful at all. If you are naturally less intuitive, you probably know what I am talking about.

So, where do you start in creating new ideas? First of all, no one can tell you where you SHOULD start. I think that is probably why artists usually share their visions and not universal truths. You can do whatever you want. You can start from any angle when you're creating or trying to solve a problem. actually, it doesn't really matter where you choose to start. Whether you need to create a solution at work, invent the next flying car, or make a short film for a friend's wedding, you can start anywhere-at the end, at the beginning, or in the middle.

It doesn't really matter where you start. What matters is when you ask where you *should* start. This shows that you're afraid. You are afraid to f*ck it up; you are afraid to not follow the right *protocol* or the right *formula*. But creativity is NOT about following the protocol. There is no formula for creativity. You want a safety net in case you fail.

I'm here to tell you there is nothing to fear. You don't need a safety net. It doesn't matter where you start because there is no *failing* in creativity. You can only learn from unexpected results. If I conceive an illusion that physically can't be done, it doesn't matter! I've made a discovery.

Let's say you have a great solution for a problem, but your boss isn't impressed? It doesn't matter! You shaped your mind to create a solution! The most important thing is giving yourself permission to try and fail, and try again while having fun along the way. Just start anywhere, even from the worst place if that is what it takes. If it is a fail, start again from a worse place.

Don't Think So Much

Why are we often paralysed when it is time to begin? We think about what we are going to create, about which solution to try and how to approach problems. We think about the consequences of our choices and then … nothing happens.

I often hear beginners say, "I think, think, think … and nothing comes!"

Perhaps thinking is the problem. When we think too much, we block ourselves. We may have too many ideas while not knowing which one to choose. The more we analyze the best idea to start with, the more paralysed we become. This is called ANALYSIS PARALYSIS.

Analysis paralysis happens when you try too hard to be smart, or you use everything you know to come up with a perfect beginning. "Perfect" is paralysing in creativity. "Good" is paralysing as well. You shouldn't care about having a perfect start because creativity is about exploring. Try going for a horrible start, and then see what inspires you.

Years ago, when I first wanted to create my own magic, I was looking for good ideas. I can tell you one thing for sure: nothing happened. I was trying too hard to be interesting; I was trying to create something smart that might impress my magician colleagues. I was playing with strengths that weren't mine. I was thinking (and overthinking) the whole process of simply starting. Overthinking at the beginning will handicap you. If you are trying to start with something "good," you are definitely "shooting your-self in your foot." This is not what creativity is about. Creativity is about throwing different types of rocks into the lake to see what kind of waves they create (this is a metaphor! You don't need to really do it!). It is about going into the jungle and cutting down branches and brush until you make a discovery. It doesn't matter where you start exploring. Indiana Jones didn't say, "Where is the perfect starting point to explore that jungle?" He went and discovered.

Maybe he didn't choose the best place to start. So what? It doesn't matter; it was an adventure! You lose more time thinking about how to be correct than in actually going for it and being wrong. Creativity is about picking a thread and slowly pulling it just to see where it leads you "(Still a metaphor)". This can be a scary thing to do at first, but if you trust yourself and your inner genie, you will always be delightfully surprised. Trust him to lead you places; trust him to explore different areas; Trust him to lead you somewhere you never expected to go. Above all, trust him without thinking so much.

Why Not Start Here?

"Not all those who wander are lost."

- J.R.R. Tolkien -

It doesn't matter if you have a good starting point. What's important is that you have something to start with that will *lead* you to other places. We will talk more on how to create connections in the next chapters, but for the moment, I have a great technique for you. This technique probably changed the lives of anyone crazy enough to try it. Are you ready for this amazing Crazytivity tool? Here it goes: Whatever you are working on, ask yourself, "Why not_____?" Complete the sentence however you'd like. Seem too simple? Who said creativity had to be complicated?

Consider this simple example: You've been asked to find ideas about selling products on the theme of "conviviality." Let's say you have so many ideas you don't know where to start and you're overthinking the whole thing. What if you tried the "Why not____" exercise? You could complete this sentence with basically anything.

Let's say you filled in the blank with the word "Christmas." Why? Why not? Whether it is a good starting point or not doesn't matter. What matters is where it leads you.

If you think "Christmas" is a bad idea because it is currently summer time, then think, *It is summer, I have to find something related to that. Why not surfing? Hmm, maybe surfing is a niche market, but it does make me think about the beach. The beach makes me think of when I went to the south of France with my family...* BOOM.

You now have images to work with for your conviviality theme: the south of France, a picnic on the beach, spending time with family, teenagers surfing, little children playing in the sand. From here, you can continue to develop these ideas and then readjust. With this technique, you can find dozens of starting points in only a minute !

I've created many illusions with this exercise. However It sounds so simple that most people don't want to try it. A while ago, I wanted to create a magic trick in which a dollar bill vanishes and reappears somewhere else. This trick has been done before, but I never liked the way it reappeared within a box or in someone's wallet. So, I looked around and saw some nuts sitting on my table. I thought, *Hey, why not nuts? Yes, let's do it.* And I did. I invented the *Dollar Bill in the Nut* magic trick. It was that simple.

If you look around and pick an object that doesn't work at all with what you have in mind, so what? Stop crying about how hard it is to be creative. Start again with something else. It's not about thinking; it's about going for it.

Free Yourself From Yourself

"Lord, free me of myself so I can please you."
- Michelangelo -

I don't remember completing one single magic show at which my family or friends didn't tell me afterward, "Yeah, it was great! But there is one thing you can improve: Let yourself go more … be more of yourself on stage!"
It would piss me off every single time because, deep down, I knew they were right. I wasn't a catastrophe as a performer, but even after years of stage practice and experience, my family still didn't see the *Butzi* on stage that they knew behind the scenes. Each performance, I tried to be more "me," but each time afterward, they'd say the same thing. It wasn't until I took a huge step out of my comfort zone (and acted completely ridiculous doing stupid jokes that I do in everyday life) that people started enjoying it. My friends and family stopped saying that I wasn't really *Butzi* on stage.

I've learned this lesson: We are our own slaves. It is not an external obstacle that gets in your way. We get in our way. Even if you are already creative, this is the reason you often can't express your inner genie. In everything I've studied and practiced (acting, magic, music, martial arts), I've learned that the fewer inhibitions you have, the more creative and efficient you are. Let this inner genie get out! Free him! Of course, this is not something you can do instantly just by rubbing a lamp. If anyone believes this, they are deluding themselves. If you listen to paralysing advice such as, "be creative," "be smart," or "just think outside the box," you may get pumped up for a week, but the excitement will vanish and nothing will remain.

Freeing yourself from yourself is a decision you make on a deep level. It should be an enjoyable, long-term process during which you make a habit of giving each idea a chance. Take your every intuition and instinct and experiment with them. Making this decision will pay off in the short term as well! Listen to yourself at any time. Every time you hear a voice within, or have an impulse to do something, or give your opinion … don't restrain yourself. Go for it!

Have you seen the movie "Yes Man!" with Jim Carrey? If not, I suggest you do. His character is forced to answer "yes" to everything, every day, in order to change his life. Although it is a hilarious film, there is also a strong message behind it: You can always do something excessively as an exercise to change habits and find a new balance in your life.

Why not do that with creativity? Every time something arises, go for it! Say yes to it!

Maybe a little voice inside you will say something like, *No, this idea is stupid. This is impossible and doesn't make sense...*

Answer that voice with, "Hey, you! You are not helping when I need to be creative! Give me a break, ok?! I know what I'm doing here. Go take a walk!"

You will progressively feel better and better. Not only will it feel good but it will also have tremendously positive effects on your life, your job, your personal relationships, and your projects.

Reject the Clichés

• Artistic or Technical?

I strongly believe that deciding whether or not you are creative is not a huge decision to make. Yes, many artistic people are creative. However, many technical people are as well in their own ways! Both types of people are equally good at being creative. Let's stop making assumptions about creative people.

Many people have an image of an artist as a crazy person who builds revolutionary art with conceptual materials— art that has a meaning the average person can't understand. Most often, this artist doesn't understand the depth of his own art himself, yet when he dies, everyone starts inventing tales about it!

Creativity is more than this idea of an artist. Creativity is in everyone, from a mathematician to a magician, from a visual artist to an engineer who knows a thousand different ways to build a wall. I forbid you to think any one type of person is more creative than you are, even if he is a painter, an inventor of awesome machines, or performs with Cirque du Soleil. We each have a precious stone inside of us that is asking to shine. It doesn't matter what color it is or what size it is— it is precious.

• Conventional or Unconventional?

Another myth about creativity is that the population can be separated into two categories: the boring conventional uncreative type and the unconventional creative type. There is an idea that conventional people can't be creative unless they learn to be completely different people. Nonsense. Of course, there is a conventional way of doing things in every structure of every society that usually doesn't help creativity, but don't think this is what blocks creativity.

I know tons of conventional guys (in their choice of job, lifestyle, in the clothes they wear) who are surprisingly creative and innovative! I know magicians with very classic magician looks that have super original minds! I also know artists and magicians who look very unconventional and rebellious, but are unoriginal in their tricks and simply copy other artists' ideas. Whatever you are labelled as, it doesn't matter. No label will prevent you from expressing and developing your ideas.

Let's Play with Your Inner Genie !

Try this: Write down two or three projects you are currently working on or that you have in mind but can't seem to get started:

-

-

-

Now, find five ridiculous places to start each one of them.
Say out loud, "Why not _____?" or "Why not start with the word_____?"
Now, explore finding five additional leads for each idea. Yes, I'm telling you that you can easily find 25 new ways to approach each project. I'm even telling you that this is possible every day.
        You want to write a movie script? Why not start with this: I'm looking around me right now and see my watch ... watch! Perhaps the main character is a master of time (this could be lead #1.) Perhaps he is in a hurry (here's lead #2.) Maybe he's a salesman selling watches (lead #3). Maybe he knows how to travel through time (lead #4).
I discovered all of these leads in less than two minutes. And also, it doesn't matter what you come up with. Just identify a starting point; your intellect will jump on some cool developments LATER. In this initial moment, you just need to start. You need to go somewhere, anywhere. Go for it !

If you are a manager, a team leader, an entrepreneur, or CEO, I have designed a special article for each chapter. To access them, simply go to my blog at this address: www.butzisblog.com

Nutshell Recap

- You are already creative, and it isn't make-believe, it's genetics.

- Take care of your inner genie. No one puts inner genie in the corner.

- Trust your magical moments and capture them.

- Creativity is a process of exploration; it doesn't matter where you begin.

- Thinking hard and trying to be smart when looking for ideas is not a good idea.

- Start anywhere, from any angle. Just let yourself lead.

- Give yourself a break from yourself!

- Whatever people say about you, don't listen to them. Anyone can be creative.

Secret #2
Reclaim
Your Childhood
Superpowers

Magician's Reveal

It's cool to know we are all naturally creative. But what time of your life were you closest to your natural state of being? When were you most in touch with your authentic self? Obviously, it was when you were a child. It is important to remember that being in touch with qualities you had when you were young will allow you to tap into your natural creativity in a deeper way.

The good news is that we are all still children, all of us! What? You thought you were an adult? Well, magicians are in the best position to tell you it isn't true. We know this because we see it all the time in our audience's eyes as they experience good magic. Important people, the most serious businessmen, high status CEOs, and politicians will give us this boyish smile and candid eye when we are performing. Whether this captivated look is for 45 minutes, or for only half a second, it is there. This childlike wonderment is in each and every one of us.

From experience, I can tell you that this look of wonderment is the purest form of yourself that is ever to shine from your beautiful eyes and face. It shows you are a candid, joyful, unworried, curious, playful, and open person. We magicians know (and any honest magician will tell you) that we were initially drawn to magic because of the childlike joy it brings; we like to play with toys and to help our audience wonder and dream again. Being a magician is a childlike profession. Our duty is to awake an audience's inner child. I am such a magician, and what I love about my job right now is that I get to help you awaken your own inner child.

Do You See that You're Still a Kid?

"The only difference between you and a kid is the years that have passed and the price of your toys."
        - A combination of quotes by unknown guys -

Some of you might be sceptical about still being childlike. Maybe you don't have the chance to see those candid eyes in this cruel world. I'm not here to convince you. I want you to discover this for yourself. I've got a little exercise for you for fun's sake:

The "Proust" Exercise

What did you love to eat and drink as a kid? Cookies and chocolate milk?
Whatever it is, go and get some. Prepare it exactly like it was prepared when you were a child. Just close your eyes, relax a bit, and take a deep breath. Now, taste it and let your thoughts go back to your childhood.
Don't try to remember anything. Just relax and let yourself feel, think, and react naturally. Chances are, you will return to your childhood as a vague feeling, a precise memory, or maybe an overall mood.
You could also try to remember the smells of your house growing up. Try remembering the voice of your childhood friends. Enjoy this for a moment.

What does this exercise teach us? Nothing really … but it is fun! Actually no, it does teach us something. It reminds us that the person reacting to this exercise is your inner child. It is still you, but it is a previous version of yourself that you've suppressed in order survive in this tough adult world. Does this remind you of someone else? Yep! Chances are your inner child and inner genie are the same person.

Though this part of you is still being acknowledged and nurtured, let it shine through in what you are already doing to create a wave of authenticity in your life. It will infiltrate your work and projects. This authenticity will translate itself into more joy, more creativity, and provide more magic for an exciting life.

Seems too simple? Maybe it is. People work hard during the year; they play the part of the responsible adult. However, as soon as they are on vacation, they do the things they loved to do as kids! They are busy with outdoor activities, curious again, play with other kids, relax, eat, are lazy, take naps and watch cartoons (okay, for the cartoons, maybe that's just me). When adults are on vacation they reconnect with their true self. The argument that there is no time to do this in "real" life is B.S. You can always take a moment during the day, or in the evening, to disconnect from the rat race and reconnect with your true self. Make the effort. It is worth it.

George Land's Creativity Test

George Land conducted in 1968 a research study to test the creative capacities of 1,600 children from age 3 to 5 years old. The test was conceived to measure the participant's capacity to create new ideas and out of the box solutions to certain problems… and it is the same one he devised for NASA to help select innovative engineers and scientists. The results on those toddlers were surprising but what he discovered next was even more so. He re-tested the same children at 10 years old, and again at 15 years old. The results amongst 3 to 5 years olds were 98%! And it dropped to only 30% when they were 10 years old! By the time they were 15 years old it dropped to 12%

So the same test was then given to 280,000 adults, and the results were… 2% !

"What we have concluded," wrote Land, "is that non-creative behavior is learned."

(Source: George Land and Beth Jarman, Breaking Point and Beyond. San Francisco: HarperBusiness, 1993)

Creativity is a Kid's Game

"Draw with a pencil, so if you mess up, you can erase it and do it again."

- Thaïs, my niece, age 5 -

What do children have to do with creativity? In my eyes, everything. In my keynote speeches and workshops, when I ask people if they think they are creative , around 10% of them raise their hands. When I ask if they think they were creative as a child, everyone will raise their hand.

When I started my career as a magician, I also decided to explore different arts and subjects to enrich my craft further. I wanted to understand the ins and outs of as many fields as I could. I trained as a clown and actor. I worked with various directors to learn about the art of filming. I worked with writers to learn about scriptwriting. I read tons of books about acting theories, theater, creativity, and entrepreneurial innovation. I practiced.

I practiced, practiced, practiced— music, magic, acting, juggling. I always went back to the theories and the wise teachings I've received to understand what it was *all about*.

And one day, as I was reading Constantin Stanislavski's collection of essays and memoirs for actors, *The Stanislavski Legacy,* one line, in particular, had a huge effect on me: "You have to study kids to learn about creativity because they are closer to nature."

This had a great impact on me, though it didn't hit me instantly; it was like a shock wave that would hit years later. It was like a seed planted in the center of my brain that I couldn't ignore as it grew. So much evolved for me from this one idea.

What did Stanislavski mean by that? I think he simply meant that children haven't yet been forged by culture and education. Therefore, they are closer to our natural state as humans, to our primitive state. And because creativity is innate, studying children puts us in touch with this amazing power we all have.

In my online creativity course, I interview my niece and nephew. I ask them about creativity, and what they say is surprisingly true and simple at the same time, just like in the above quote from my niece. I asked her for advice on how to be creative and start a project, and her response always feels like a slap in the face!

Find your inner child's powers, and you will get back your creative powers!

To learn more about retracing your childhood spirit, you can watch my TEDx "Butzi's TEDx on how to find back your Childlike Spirit" on my Youtube Channel, "Butzi, Speaker & Magician."

Superpower #1: Being a Sponge

*"**Be like a sponge when it comes to each new experience.
If you want to be able to express it.**"*

- Jim Rohn -

I believe creativity is very much like a sponge: you absorb, and then you squeeze it out. Techniques to "squeeze it out" are just as important as the ones to absorb. In the absorption process, your brain will be connecting new elements to old ones, as well as connecting the new elements with each other. This is how you *nourish* your creative brain. Look at children. They are always learning and absorbing. Children are open-minded to everything and everyone. They're constantly curious about how stuff around them works.

We can do all of this too but on the next level! Just because we know how things work on a superfluous level doesn't mean we have to stop there! Do you know how a plane flies? Kind of. Go further, learn more, absorb more! Doing so will allow you to make more connections with your environment (as we are going to see in the chapter about connections). I am asking you to wonder, to dig deeper, to ask yourself questions. This will help you absorb more.

And then, squeeze it out without caring. Not caring what other people think of your ideas and your projects is essential in the process of freeing yourself from yourself. Don't worry about tools and techniques for the moment because having this attitude is so much more important! Kids have it. Ask a child to draw their mother on a piece of paper, and they'll draw four horrible lines using five different colors, while simultaneously drawing on your table with a big smile on their face. They don't care if it looks horrible— they just get it out. They don't care of what other people might say.

I once asked my five-year-old niece and my six-year-old nephew if they were thinking of what people might say about their drawings while they were drawing them. They didn't know what I was talking about. They both responded with, "No, what's most important is that I like it."

Children don't think of the things that often block adults in the creative process. They are simply having fun and creating for themselves. Get an opinion detox before developing, polishing, and using your experience to create. Like a sponge, squeeze it out and express your ideas! If you want to have fun and express yourself, I've created a Facebook group, The Crazytivity Club, as a place for you to do so. Come and share your crazy thoughts and ideas while helping your fellow creators in the Crazytivity community! (@thecrazytivityclub)

Superpower #2: Dreaming

"Hey! The world needs dreamers, Luke. Never stop licking things."

- Phil Dunphy, Modern Family -

We had such huge dreams when we were children! We wanted to be astronauts, firemen, skateboarding world champions, and more. As time went by, little by little, we stopped. I know why. If you dream, you might get attached to your goal and be disappointed if you don't make it. The bigger your dreams are, the shittier you might feel about your life if you don't achieve them. It can be depressing awaiting the outcome of our dreams. Schools try to format children. Parents and teachers "protect" their kids by telling them to stop dreaming, to "come back to reality." They don't want their child to be disappointed.

Even if they have good intentions, I feel this is not the right thing to do. This can have terrible consequences on our creativity and actions as adults. We don't want to be deceived, so we aim low and do what others do. We don't dare to go for originality because we're afraid of being criticized. But when you stop dreaming, you become a follower. You copy what others do just to be safe. You and I both know this is not the right way to be on a creative track.

Here is the secret: You don't need to believe that all of your dreams will come true. Allowing yourself to dream, and give each dream a chance, doesn't mean you will succeed at bringing all of them into reality. Dreaming as much as you want doesn't take time or cost money… above all it is fun! Dreaming challenges you to create and improve as a person. It helps you set bigger goals, so you can reach those dreams. If you don't dream, you will always go for monotonous and boring projects. You will never create amazing projects; you will never make a difference in this world.

As magicians, we create amazing and extravagant dreams that always seem impossible so that we can amaze you. Not all of our crazy ideas will make it to reality, but we don't care. We believe in our stupid ideas until we can bring them (well, at least some of them) to reality. The remaining dreams are like people you love that live abroad: They are not here, but you love them; you keep in touch with them sometimes. You can have big dreams as well. You can set high goals and still be okay if you don't achieve all of them.

Let's try this: Sit down every day, set a timer to three minutes (so you don't have to keep an eye on the time) and daydream about anything you want! Don't think about realistic things— just let it go!»

Superpower #3: Carelessness

"Just keep moving forward and don't give a shit about what anybody thinks. Do what you have to do, for you."
                                                              - Johnny Depp -

Caring about other people's judgment has everything to do with ego, an overused and tricky word with many definitions. The Cambridge Dictionary's definition of ego is that it's your conscious mind; it is the part of your identity that you define as your "self." The Oxford Dictionary defines it as your sense of self-esteem and self-importance.

However, ego doesn't define you. It is who you think you are. It is how you see yourself. Because we are social beings, we can easily see ourselves through the eyes of others. We often put too much importance in this sense of self-importance.

Children don't care what others think of them, especially before they turn seven. They instinctively know we are, in fact, a piece of dust in this vast universe. When we care too much about what others think of us, we lose our authenticity and give others the power to make us what they'd like us to be. When this happens, our creativity decreases at the same rate our fear of being judged increases. This is approximatively the time your inner genie is asked to go in the corner and not move too much.

If you want to stop caring what other people think of your crazy ideas, you need to work on that. You can start by using a simple, everyday tool to tame your ego. Dissociate yourself from your ego and tame it every day. It is a trick of the imagination and nothing more. Whenever you see yourself repressing something you really want to do, or when you see yourself doing something that is not *really you*, pause, breathe, and ask yourself: What should I really be doing here? "What do I really want to do?"

Instead of thinking about what others would like you to do, listen to your gut. Listen to what you feel *you* should do… what you want to do.

It took me quite a while to get the feel of what bargaining with my ego really meant. However, I see it clearly now. Ego is necessary; it is vital— and you can't get rid of it. When you hear that a person has no ego, it is an exaggeration. Ego is too often in our way in the society we live in. We want to show off to others; we want to prove ourselves and project a distorted image of this *self* to others. However, this stands in the way of creativity.

You must become an ego tamer and deal with the beast every day. Each time it roars, don't fight it or try to ignore it. Acknowledge it, and answer it with something like: "I know you are hungry, but we have talked about it, you are on a diet now."

Superpower #4: Boldness

"I have no idea what I am doing, but incompetence has never prevented me from plunging in with enthusiasm."

- Woody Allen -

Would you carelessly play with a dog that is the same size as you? Would you eat flowers just to see what they taste like? Kids would. (I can also tell you that daisies don't really taste of anything.)

A child won't sit at a table and think hard on how to solve a problem. He touches things. He picks up your lipstick and paints on the floor with it. I actually did this when I was a very cute blonde, two-year-old angel. Was it a bad idea? Maybe in the context (a rented apartment for the holidays). However, it might not have been if I were an experimental artist in search of inspiration.

We can all learn from this attitude if we reframe it in a professional context. No one can tell you that what you have in mind is a good or bad idea until you try it. Maybe it is a bad idea, but it might teach you a lesson that will lead you to a creative breakthrough. You will never know until you try.

We've been taught to avoid risks for our own security and protection. This avoidance helps us have a passable life in society. However, fearing risk often prevents us from trying things out. Taking risks will push you into creating something new; it helps you discover places no one has been before. Taking risks will lead you to life lessons and breakthroughs. Risks trigger your brain to create connections with unseen situations and surprises that are waiting just beyond your comfort zone.

And yes, it is often risky to try new things. However, now you are old enough to measure the risks for yourself. Yes, you may lose time, money, or the good image of what people think of you. Every lesson has a price. If you want to learn and push yourself out of your comfort zone, you might expect to invest a bit of time and money. You may even shock a few people. The trick is to understand that you can't fail. you can only learn.

Have you ever seen a baby think of failure? Failure doesn't exist to a baby. He doesn't read a book on how to walk; he just tries and fails horribly. This bit of pain teaches him something, and then he tries something else, but he never doubts that he is going to succeed. Babies instinctively know it is only a matter of time before they succeed and that each failure is also a step toward their success. We can all apply this fearlessness in our own projects instead of complaining that something didn't work (complaining is the grown-up version of crying!)

The Guy Who Wrote this Book is Still a Kid

Though I have the numerical age of an adult, I'm pretty sure I'm still a kid. Sometimes, I wake up and watch cartoons with my breakfast. At times, when things are getting serious, I have this burning energy in my stomach to play and make a joke. I need to make the serious work enjoyable and fun. I go to magic shops because it is not appropriate anymore for me to visit kid's toy stores. I love to play and to laugh and I love eating chocolate. When kids see me, they instantly know I'm one of them. Just seconds after we meet, we're playing together inventing weird screams. Even the name I go by, Butzi, is a nickname my German family gave me.

In our German dialect, Butzi means "little kid," or "little Todd." Traditionally, we name the last child of the family, "the little one," which was the case for me. This nickname was a way for me to keep my childish spirit.

When it came time to pick a magician's name (Johannes Alinhac is just impossible to remember) I picked Butzi. I brainstormed for hours on other ridiculous and cheesy magician names, but my parents even agreed, Butzi was it. It was like one of those obvious things that is right under your eyes, but you can't see it because it seems too simple.

After a year of performing magic here and there, I discovered that magic is a great way to re-awaken everyone's inner child. I decided that "Reawakening the Inner Child" would be my mantra. Suddenly, everything clicked: The childhood nickname I'd chosen to be my magician name aligned with my mantra. It all made sense to me. With the help of my inner child, I set out on a mission to help others bring joy into their lives by awakening the inner child within them.

It was later in my life, when I became involved in theater, acting, improvisation, filming, and editing, that I started working on creativity. I then began coaching others. However, throughout this time, my mantra didn't change one bit. I thought that I should change it, but it didn't feel right. As I said before, the single most important thing in being creative is reconnecting with your inner child. I kept my nickname and continue to use it as a speaker, magician, writer, and for everything else.

I've decided to live my life by constantly nurturing my inner child. I will always strive to find the best ways to incorporate it into my professional and personal life, and then share my thoughts with others.

Kids Aren't the Only Ones with Imagination

We have just as much imagination now as we did when we were kids.

Whaaaaaaat?

Yes, that is what I said: I don't think that children have more imagination than adults. How can this be after everything I have said? Children are super creative and full of imagination, this is true. I believe that they are masters of letting their imagination flow, but is not that they can imagine *more* things— it is that they let their minds wander more freely. They create more with less. We were born the same way.

I strongly believe that imagination can't be quantified; it is potential energy that can be developed. Someone with a great deal of imagination is someone who can expand their thoughts and visions. I believe that, as adults, we have a higher potential of imagination because we have more experiences that have accumulated in our minds throughout the years. We have seen, thought, and achieved much more than a child. We have more ideas and more crazy thoughts flowing in our minds. However, somewhere along the way, we began to block our imagination. We began to segment our ways of thinking and to use common patterns of thought. We don't think it is possible to let our imagination flow like children do. We don't develop our imagination's potential. Because children do things differently, it seems they have more potential than we do.

So, follow the kids' lead! Take whatever is in your head and expand it to a higher degree just when your habit is to unconsciously block it. Start this now, because the less we practice this, the worse we become at letting our imagination flow and pushing our creative capabilities. Here is an example of how to do it:

Let's Play With Our Natural Imagination !

I suggest we do what kids love to do the most: PLAY. Even more, let's play with our imaginations.

So far, I've been saying that children use their imagination without barrier. Give a box of Legos to a six year old, and he will build a weird and never-before-seen structure that he can easily discuss for ten to thirty minutes:

"So that is the castle[...] but crocodiles took it over[...] and Sophie can't go inside because of this car with no wheels that blocks the entrance and..."

Imagine having that ability again but with your own set of skills, knowledge, discipline, and experience. Wouldn't that be amazing?! I suggest we use my favorite tool of all time to create illusions, movies, and stupid games.

Here is the question to answer: Wouldn't it be cool if_____?

I love this question because it takes all seriousness and pressure off your shoulders; it gives space for your inner child to play around.

Pick a theme, a project you are working on, something about the way you live your life, or even an issue in the world, then write down that question: Wouldn't it be cool if_____? Now, I'm going to set the rules of this little game. You are NOT allowed to do the following:

-Think about the viability of your ideas.
-Think about how you are going to achieve them.
-Think that your idea is stupid.
-Think about the next thing you are going to write.

The four items on this list are the things that most commonly block your imagination. This is because when you were growing up, frustrated or worried grown-ups would tell you, "Don't be silly," or "Come on, be realistic," or "Think hard," or "Don't expect too much, you might be disappointed." We have all heard this at some point. These comments are a hidden defect that will directly kill the capacity to expand your imagination.

Now that you have written down that question, you are going to list 20 things that would be cool, whatever cool means for you. I ean toward the sense of amazing. I know it sounds like a big task, but remember this is an exercise to expand your imagination. If you start with just one idea, then another one will appear, and you'll continue to come up with even more, step by step. It will be easy!

Ready? GO FOR IT!

What Actors Can Teach You About Imagination

"Being an actor is the loneliest thing in the world. You are all alone with your concentration and imagination, and that's all you have."
                                                        - James Dean -

Actors are super creative, even if we don't see it while watching them on screen. When you see an actor fighting a dinosaur in a movie, he is, in fact, performing in front of a green screen while people holding cameras, clip boards, and microphones are watching. You see the character crying because something in the scene has reminded him of his dead father. In reality, an actor is looking at an ugly wall with a bearded guy standing behind a light. The actor's father is actually healthy and he has no reason to cry. He is probably super happy to be at work.

So how do actors do this? They imagine. They create a situation in their minds. Actors have learned to imagine people, surroundings, and even emotions. This is all something we did naturally as kids. You wanted an ice cream? That stake was high enough to have you crying on demand! Actors re-learned to have such reactions by getting rid of blocks and barriers holding back their already existing imagination. You can do this too. It is a long-term process it will take a little bit of work each day, but it can be fun. You can achieve this by using grand master Stanislavski's advice. This legendary theatre teacher largely influenced the acting landscape by basing his acting system on the "magic if."

He told his actors to ask themselves, "What would I do IF I was in this situation?"

You can use this tool as well. A great way to create ideas by exercising your imagination is to ask yourself, What if _____? and then complete the sentence. Because you are who you are, because you are unique, because of your personal interests, your experience, your life story, unique ideas are going to appear *magically*.

Try this: Write down a problem, a theme, or even a single word. Begin writing a series of sentences with "What if," without trying to be smart. This tool, as easy as it looks, is one of the strongest tools in creativity. It has been scientifically proven that the same region in the brain is stimulated whether you are dreaming, imagining a situation, or experiencing something in the real world. Imagination is the "next best thing" after reality! Don't underestimate it! You can also start with these kind of sentences:

-"What if I were_____? What would I do?"
-"What if I were a magician, what would I do?"
-"What if I had superpowers ?"
-"What if I could ?"
-"If I didn't care about how to achieve my dreams, I would___"
-"What if I were Einstein, or Dalai Lama, what would I do?"

Knowledge as a Weapon

"Knowledge is to creativity what a sword is to martial arts."
- Butzi (yep, that's me) -

What about knowledge? Kid's don't have that! Ha! Ever thought of that?

How can kids be creative if they don't know anything? They should be dumb. Well, even if some of them are, they are probably still super creative. Knowledge is not necessary for creativity, just as it is not necessary for a fighter to have a weapon to fight. The fighter is the weapon. It is the same with creativity. You don't need a weapon (in this case, your knowledge) to be efficient. However, if you use the knowledge you do have in combination with your fighting skills (your inner genie, your inner child), it can provide you with a huge advantage. Your knowledge is still a very important element when it comes to creativity. Using it will allow you to have results you wouldn't be able to achieve otherwise.

Some may argue that not having a frame of reference or knowledge on the subject may give you a "fresh look." I do agree. But whether you are an engineer or painter, if you lack specific technique or knowledge in your field, chances are, you are not going to create miracles, even if you have a fresh look. Concentrate on reconnecting with your inner child for that fresh state of mind, and the rest will come easily.

Having said that, we have to admit that without knowledge, you might waste time searching for methods that already exist. For example, if you are designing a new smartphone, and you don't know about the latest nano chip, you might miss out on hundreds of possibilities and opportunities. You don't want to be stuck in one spot in your work forever thinking, "I wish we could make this phone smaller or stronger, but today's technology doesn't allow it."

When you know more about your subject, it gives your brain more starting points for different tracks of thinking. Knowledge prevents you from believing you have reached a technical dead-end.

The more you know about the subject, the easier and the faster it will be for you to be original and innovative. Your brain makes thousands of connections from every single angle, consciously and unconsciously, when you are looking for a solution. This is only possible if you have a childlike attitude. As a magician, the more I know about gimmicks, techniques, subtleties, and different types of magical effects, the faster my brain can create connections— the faster it can combine different elements to create an original method. But if I can't dream the way a kid dreams, then what is the point?

Find Your Inner Child's Balance

"Creativity is a combination of discipline and a childlike spirit."

- Robert Green -

Adopting a childlike attitude is not all or nothing. Having this attitude is not about crawling around, running naked on the beach, or crying for a cookie (well, you could do this if you want... it's none of my business). In adopting a child's attitude, you don't have to become a magician or abandon everything you used to do all at once. It is about taking the good components of a childlike perspective and slowly incorporating it into your life. It's about reframing what you are currently working on with a new outlook. It is about finding balance, reaching the right dosage of your serious and responsible qualities with the right amount of your childlike ones.

Take the useful attitudes we all had naturally when we were young, get rid of your filters, reclaim your super-powers, and mix them with your experiences and your knowledge. You can still have a great idea if you don't know all the specific details of a subject — your attitude is most important. If you use this attitude in your personal and professional life, your creativity will skyrocket. It might take some time to find the right balance, but it will come.

Einstein, the Dalai Lama, and Obama each have a childlike dispositions. You see them doing silly things, sticking out their tongues, saying funny quotes, having fun for no reason. They've often told us imagination is the most important thing.

"If I had to name my greatest strength, I guess it would be my humility. Greatest weakness, it's possible that I'm a little too awesome."

- Barack Obama, at the 2008 Al Smith Dinner -

These childlike qualities and skills are natural; they will come back to you every day if you let them.

If you are a manager, a team leader, an entrepreneur, or CEO, I have designed a special article for each chapter. To access them, simply go to my blog at this address: www.butzisblog.com

Nutshell Recap

- Whether you want it or not, you are still a kid inside.

- Acknowledging your inner child will skyrocket your creativity.

- You are naturally bold, curious, and crazy— don't block it!

- Falling and standing up again is the best way to learn about creativity.

- You don't need "more" imagination, you need fewer barriers.

- Dream like a kid to set high goals.

- EGO might be in your way. Make it an ally, not an enemy.

- Learn to play seriously and to have fun at work.

- Use the Stanislavski tool: the magic "if" to create crazy ideas.

- Knowledge is a great weapon, but you aren't a creative warrior without your childlike spirit.

- Reconnect with your inner child, and mix the amazing qualities with your experience and knowledge.

Secret #3
Overcome Your obstacles and Fear

Magician's Reveal

I was at my parents' house, playing in my room with my props (told you I was a kid), when I had one of my first ideas. I decided to reinvent a rope routine I had just learned. I would use the same sleights of hand as the original routine, but I would use a neck tie instead of ropes to invent a new twist on the story around it. I would address the fact that it is a pain not knowing how to tie a neck tie, and so on.

Looking back, I can say it was a great idea. However I didn't do the routine at the time. I avoided it. I'd find excuses for myself such as, *I'm sure it was done before, it's not that impressive after all.*

I had hundreds of other ideas that I stopped developing and abandoned in a notepad that I eventually threw away. Why did I do this? After a few years of overcoming my fears and gaining confidence, I now know why: It was a lack of self-esteem; the fear of what people would think about what I'd created; the fear of being criticized; the fear of looking stupid. The crazy part was that, in the moment, I was a 100% sure that my excuses were legitimate. I could have sworn they were. I could logically explain why my ideas were too stupid or impossible to be used and developed.

However, something happened. I couldn't forget the tie illusion I had in mind. I thought, "Maybe, you know? I should try it out."

One day, I took all my courage and told myself to do it, even if it felt stupid. I constructed it and showed it to my sister. As supportive as she always is, she said she loved it. I showed it to my mother, but you know mothers. She would have loved it even if it was horrible. So, I showed it to my skeptical father. He liked it. However, I still didn't perform it publicly for a while.

One day, I finally decided to try it out in front of an audience. People really appreciated it! I was still surprised! I did it again and again until I gained enough confidence to perform it at the Magic Castle in Los Angeles. I've even published the illusion in a magazine and in my book that I wrote for other magicians.

Now that I remember all of this, I feel ridiculous. I lost so much time being worried about what other people would think of me and on fishing for approval. Emotional and mental energy was lost because of self-doubt. If I had such an idea today, it would go through the express highway: Idea -> Captured -> Develop it -> Test it -> Act on it.

This experience taught me a valuable lesson— There never really was an actual obstacle to building and performing this illusion. Like all of the tricks and performances I've thought of, I'd built these obstacles in my mind. Overcoming the fear of sharing my ideas (thankfully) gave me courage to go further and gain confidence in the ones to follow.

We all know this story because we've all experienced it. I'm sure it has happened with a random idea you had, a side project you thought of, or with anything else you wanted to create. However, we are masters at building mental illusions, obstacles, fears, blocks, excuses, you name it. We avoid giving life to too many of our best ideas.

I'm here to tell you not to feel bad about it. Don't feel bad because we all create these unfounded illusions. A good magician knows how to spot an illusion when he sees one. And when we know how the trick is done; the illusion vanishes, it all becomes obvious. I want you to be able to see through these illusions of self-doubt as well. If I can do it, you can do it too.

Do You Really Need a Safety Net?

When I studied acting in London with Ewa Kolodzjieska, a great acting teacher, I learned a valuable lesson about creativity and freeing myself by overcoming fears. As an actor, I was terrified to play a character without knowing how in advance. I knew the lines, sure, but had no idea how to create an interesting way of saying them.

I remember this day when Ewa asked another actor and me to create a scene in which the characters where named "A" and "B." We were free to decide how the scene would unfold; we chose the setting, the purpose of dialogue, even the sex of the characters. Because we were given such freedom of options, I felt even more pressure for the scene to be "good." Before we began, I asked my teacher, "So, we don't know how this will work out at all? No structure, no safety net?"

I was expecting a logical explanation, but she answered, "Yes. But it will be fun!" I didn't know what to say. I smiled. Our scene unfolded, and it was indeed a lot of fun. We created characters and plot and gave our actions 100% of our imagination. Even if we knew they weren't the best choices we could have made, it didn't matter. We went for it with no fear; we played like little kids.

When other partners in the class had given it a shot, their ideas were completely different than ours— but were also fun! No scenes were *better* than the next; they were each original and unique. No one ended up needing the safety net we thought we would need.

When I came home from this workshop, I wrote on a piece of paper, "No safety net is fun." I pinned it to the wall next to my desk.

This was one of the biggest and most liberating creative breakthroughs I'd experienced. I got rid of this unfounded fear of the unknown by looking at the illusion from another direction. I also began to understand that freedom can be scary.

We say we want and love freedom, but humans, in fact, love their own limitations. We build systems and processes to reassure us and to help us avoid jumping into the unknown. Where does this fear often come from? It comes from the fear of not being *good*. We've been taught at school that this is *good* and that is *bad*. We've been handed the grade C-. The teacher is going to tell your parents you are a bad student and you are going to be grounded. No wonder we are often paralysed to try something we're unsure about after this upbringing. However, acknowledging that fear helps us get to the next step: doing something about it. It helps us to "take our courage with two hands," a saying we have in France, and jump into the unknown. Acknowledging our fear will help us discover what can be discovered.

My clown teacher used to say, "Do something, anything. It doesn't matter if it is bad." Top magicians are able to create fantastic tricks from horrible ideas by using this principle. Artists do amazing things by using their mistakes as a springboard. Sometimes, the most successful, creative people have no idea what they are doing when they start out, but they understand there is no risk in exploration. Even when you fail, you discover. You learn from each step. Realizing that I don't need a safety net (and that it's actually more fun without one) helped me create more magic tricks, presentations, and videos.

Most of our fears are logically unfounded. However, we often have an instinctive reflex toward fear of the unknown. It is a reflex of survival from the time wild animals would chase us to eat us. If you are reading this book, it seems unlikely that you live in an environment where pumas and lions can chase you at any time and yet we are still afraid that something terrible might happen! From now on, when you start a painting, a project, or any other innovative endeavor, just start without caring what will happen. Let one object inspire you and work from there. Let one thought lead you to another one. It might be "good," it might be "bad." It doesn't matter how it turns out because you had fun exploring. Be crazy enough to just go for it. It takes courage, and that is why you need to do it. You know you should.

Failure Doesn't Exist

"An essential aspect of creativity is not being afraid to fail."
- Edwin Land -

In playing the "A and B scene" activity in my acting class (and in several other experiences in my life) I discovered that once you go for it without fear and with positive energy, you get great results and discoveries. Once you are finished, you realize it wasn't that bad after all.

I understand that starting without fear is easier said than done. But what are we really afraid of? Most of the time, people say they are afraid to "fail" in one form or another. You may fear the failure of not receiving your boss's approval or the failure of not having great ideas. You may fear the failure of disappointment or the failure of not pleasing others.

I must tell you this: Failure is an invented concept. It doesn't exist. We created the term "failing" to have a binary outcome and to make things easier to understand. In his book, *Poke the Box* (which I highly recommend), Seth Godin talks about this concept. I learned even more about this concept as a teenager training in judo.

For those who aren't familiar, judo is a Japanese martial art in which to win, the opponent must be thrown onto his back... and hitting is forbidden. To simplify, we could say "winning" is when your opponent falls on his back, and "losing" is when you fall on yours.

Now, does it mean that if you fall on your back during a fight you are a "loser" and you "failed" to win? Not if you are in a competition with yourself.

I was lucky to find good teachers. They always taught me that it doesn't matter how many times you fall, what matters is how many times you stand up. Each time you fall you learn something. Each time you stand up you put into practice what you've learned until you fall again. It is a painful but virtuous circle. I know this has been said many times, but trust me, when every muscle in your body hurts but you still stand up, you embody that lesson. When I was sixteen years old, two friends and I trained in Japan for a month. We trained for three hours each day. I was five to eight years younger than the other boys, and I was ridiculously skinny. Each session, we'd complete around thirteen fights, each lasting nine minutes. It was hard as hell. We fought on a floor made of straw that the instructors would water in the morning. Do you see where I'm going with this? Yes, I fell a lot. If I were to do some math, I'd say I fell six times per fight. That adds up to 1,440 falls in a month. In one fight, I remember throwing a guy to the floor only once, and he threw me seven times after.

I cried when the month was over. I wanted to quit judo. I was too skinny anyways, and my defence skills weren't developed (these were my excuses anyways). However, my friends helped me remember that I always needed to stand back up, and so I did. I put my ego in my back pocket, and I persevered.

When I came back to France, something fun happened: I defeated people that were kicking my ass before I went to Japan. I couldn't see it, but I'd actually became much stronger. I changed strategies; I went from a right-handed fighter to a left-handed fighter. It took me months, but I relearned all the techniques differently. With time, I started winning more fights and competitions, and I began to have fun with it. I stopped whining and allowed myself to learn lessons from each experience. To spell out this "winner" and "loser" analogy, being a loser is to stay on the floor and quit when you fall. I didn't.

I tell this story because it is so similar with creativity. It doesn't matter if you fail to have good ideas 100 times or 1,440 times a month. What matters is that you go for it 100%, and that you never get discouraged from your failures. That 1,441st time you try is when you might have the best idea that anyone has ever had. It could be an innovative business model, a new function to an already existing product, or a revolutionary idea for your art. There are countless successful entrepreneurs who failed many times before they succeeded. Actually, no successful entrepreneur or creator would ever say, "It was a hell of a smooth ride, I never failed, and everything went well."

There are always horrible failures and rejections behind each enterprise. It is normal to fail, and it is natural to find success after failures as we learn along the way. However, there is also no point pretending we are not afraid. This would just be denial. Everyone is afraid. However it is okay to be afraid. The difference between so called "geniuses" and every one else is that geniuses go for it. For example, when I go surfing, I'm afraid to face the waves. But when I speak with other surfers, they say that they are afraid as well— and the fear is what they love! It is a game of fear and courage. When you take the leap, fear disappears. You are saying, "I see you, fear, and it is okay. I'm still going in." At that point, fear has no reason to exist anymore.

So why did we invent this concept of failure? I think it was because we humans like to cut through the noise to understand where we stand in this complex world. We simplify things into "good or bad," "success or failure." I think it was a mistake to invent these concepts because it doesn't take into account the benefits of failing. Failing is a blessing; we learn so much In the process.

Juan Tamariz, a master Spanish magician, once said, "A show without three mistakes is not a good show."

When I was starting out as a magician, I didn't understand this. I tried to make as few mistakes as possible. At some point, I wondered if he was suggesting I try to make mistakes. After learning it the hard way, I understood I shouldn't try to make mistakes, but if one happened, it was a blessing. I believe this is a good way to summarize everything I have learned about the fear of failing:

Go for it 100%, using fear as a boosting energy. If you make mistakes, it is a blessing because it means you are learning.

What if I'm Rejected?

"Rejection is the greatest aphrodisiac."

- Madonna -

Aaaaah…that sweet feeling of being told our idea is stupid. I remember when I had my first job as a resident magician in a nice coastal town in Ecuador. I put together a twenty-minute act that I was proud of. After a week of performing it each night, the artistic director of the place asked to have a talk with me. At the time, I didn't speak Spanish very well, and she didn't really speak English. She mimed what she was trying to say.
She said, "Your show…como se dice…" and then she yawned in exaggeration.

My heart was instantly broken. It was rude, harsh, and inconsiderate— but I love her in retrospect. I made choice after that: I was not going to cry about it for the rest of my life saying, «creativity is not for me», but I would start getting to work and readjust whatever it was that made this show, como se dice…boring. Being rejected pushed me to create something better and to work harder. It was an opportunity. Don't get me wrong, getting rejected is the number one killer of fun at all times. When it happens to me, even today, I don't feel like talking about my ideas ever again— until I go home, tame my ego, and tell myself there is something to take from that rejection.

The good news is, this doesn't only happen to me or to you. It happens to everyone. No creative or inventive person has never been rejected. Actually, an interesting fact observed throughout human history is that most famous inventors and geniuses have been rejected more times compared to normal people. Edison invented thousands of things, but the light bulb was the success. Countless entrepreneurs, artists, and inventors have been rejected. Van Gogh wasn't even appreciated when he was living. Tim Ferris, a famous author, was rejected by 26 publishing houses before one of his books became a best seller. There are movies that weren't even financed until they become classics. You and I are not the only ones to experience rejection.

How is it that so many creators persevere while the average person stops at the first rejection? Because they know it is not their intelligence that is at stake. They know it doesn't mean they are not inventive or creative. It is not about them being "not enough," but about the idea being impractical, too expensive, or not thoroughly developed.

To rationalize this fear of rejection, ask yourself: How many ideas can you have in a day? Yes, a LOT. If you come up with ten interesting ideas when you sit and brainstorm, and nine get rejected. So what? Does that mean you are stupid? Does it mean you aren't inventive enough? No! You can always improve these ideas or go find new ones. It is all about adjusting and accepting the critics. The single thing you have to do is have fun trying. When you have fun, you don't ask yourself if you are smart enough, or if the problem is you, you just create constantly and learn in an amusing flow.

Problems Are Part of Creativity

"Solving problems should be a joy, a welcome challenge to our creativity."

- Deepak Chopra -

I would be lying if I said that if you only believe anything is possible, that the world is a piece of cake, and all obstacles are illusions. And I am not a liar. Well, only when I perform magic. Believing and dreaming freely is the first step to any project, and we have learned how to do this in the previous chapters. After this first stage, problems are going to appear, real problems and not just illusions. You may not have the necessary techniques to draw the idea you have in mind. You may not have the engineering skills to build that flying car. It might not be possible to create the educational program you've been working on. If you want to send a rocket into space, dreaming and smiling is not going to be enough. These new problems might be annoying and take time to solve; they may be impossible to solve. With that said, there are two traps you shouldn't fall into if you don't want to be stuck for the rest of your life:

1) Mistaking a real problem with a fake problem.

Double and triple check to see if your problem is a real problem, or if you are just not believing in yourself. To do this, ask yourself, What would [insert the name of a genius here] have done? If you think he would have gone for it, even if he didn't have the skill set, then apply Richard Branson's philosophy, "Screw it, let's do it."

2) If you think it is a real problem, don't back off...solve it!

I know it sounds easy to say, but I discovered throughout years of creating magical effects that a problem is almost never impossible to solve, even if you aren't a genius. tell yourself, "I'm not a genius, but I'm not an idiot." You are far from it.

I'm going to tell you a secret: When I read De Bono's

books on creativity, I loved it but was incapable of solving the little exercises that he planted here and there for the reader to understand his theories. I understood the general concept of the book, but I felt very stupid not being able to see what he could (and apparently should) see, like the fact that "one ' T ' is formed from two ' I ' s ", or that there was a smarter way to link the points between those dots. If I were to take an IQ test, my results would probably be shitty. So, I don't take the test! Problem solved!

I always find it a bit tricky to talk about problems when talking about creativity because I'm afraid to scare people away from creating and, as said in the beginning, the best thing you can do is to dream crazy and start exploring to find solutions.

But get this: Solving problems can be done in a fun way !

You don't have to be a logical genius or have a high IQ to solve problems. How is this possible? This will all unfold in this chapter and in the next one, so don't worry— I've got ya! I have plenty of tools to help you. But for now, I want to tell you this: If you don't trust yourself as a problem solver, we are on the same page. This is what blocked me for many years. I was horrible at solving problems (such as those mathematical problems in school and those infernal riddles). I didn't feel like trying because I knew I would fail. However, at some point, I stopped thinking so negatively. Stopping this thought pattern brought me the confidence to continue trying. Soon enough, I understood there is nothing complicated about generating solution, or even turning problems into solutions. It's just that other people made it look so complicated that I was afraid of it. The answer is learning to deal with the problem in a way that suits you.

For me to realize problem solving is fun, I had to start thinking about it as an idea-generating process, versus thinking about it in a logical way. Just create a volume of solutions and don't look at the quality.
Let's say you want to create an app, and you have two problems.

The first problem is that versions of the app already exist, and the second is you don't have a developer. There are two ways to act here:

a) Sit and think hard about the perfect solution.
b) Generate 70 crazy ideas in five minutes, then stop and narrow it down to the most interesting leads.

Which one sounds more fun? You know the answer (B)! And that is what we are going to learn in the next chapters. But before we get there, I want to help you get rid of your fears and to not see problems…as problems. It can be fun and helpful! This is how…

Constraints Stimulate Your Creativity

"Constraints inspire creativity. When our backs are against the wall, we come up with amazing things.".
- Biz Stone , – Co-founder Twitter -

There is a popular belief that we are more creative when we are free to do whatever we want. Despite the fact that each artist or entrepreneur would have a different opinion on the subject, only few would disagree.
Imagine you are sentenced to die. Now name your last meal. Not so easy, is it? It is difficult because you have so many choices, but you want to find your favorite meal. We have to be careful believing that freedom of thought will bring original ideas. This is a trap we can easily fall into; we get paralysed with too many choices and have no idea where to start. (P.S. I suggest eating something spicy, fatty, or heavy because you won't have to worry about digestion.)
        The paradox is that creativity is a form of freedom. You can create what you want and what you imagine, the way you want it to exist. But, weirdly enough, your brain finds better solutions when it is limited. What limitations am I talking about?

This is how it might play out for a magician. Let's say I'm hired to do a cabaret show every Thursday night for an audience that is made up of 80% corporate executives. In this one tiny sentence, I already have a dozen pre-set limitations! But it doesn't mean I'm not free to create something fun and original! I also have only 12- 20 minutes on stage, I have to choose mind blowing pieces, and therefore, I don't really have time for in-between routines and long stories. I have to bear in mind that these executives are probably getting out of work because it is a Thursday night, so I want to do something punchy, at least at the beginning. I don't want to seem too complicated but will still need to create a story in my banter. There are so many things to consider!

Here is how I can stimulate my creativity: by asking myself the right questions! What subjects or types of magic would forty-year-old executives identify with? What about the rest of the audience? Can I make a gentle joke about them because they are the minority in the room?

When I find an answer, I dig deeper. I would love a joke about a business suit jacket. What can I do? How can I borrow a jacket from an audience member without having to pull them on stage to save some time? Can I use a neck-tie? Maybe I could start with my tie routine so I speak their language. Maybe then, they would relate to me more easily from the beginning. The more I dig, the more I work with what I want and don't want, what I can do and can't do, the more original and interesting the show will be.

For those of you who work in an office, or even as a freelancer for a picky client, you have limitations, constraints, and problems! It is normal. However, if you see these constraints as opportunities to find fun solutions by playing around with them, it changes the game! Look at twitter: 140 characters. Wow, that is some limitation! Deal with that!

You can even set limitations for yourself when you are completely free! The most important thing is to define what you want to achieve as precisely as possible each step of the way. Each time you are setting constraints about your final goal and the way you will achieve it, you will get a better perspective on where you are heading.

When Are Constraints Too Restricting ?

Sometimes, in our creative process, we get stuck facing a problem and…wait, let me rephrase that: Sometimes we *think* we
are stuck facing a problem and don't know how to find a way
out. It happens to everyone and not only in magic. We get stuck
for many reasons, but it often happens when we have too many
limitations and constraints. If you panic or give up when you
face them, it may be because you just aren't used to them. Experienced innovators don't worry at all when that happens to
them. They know it is just a phase of their creative process; they
know it's just the start of another phase.

Let's look at the curve I have illustrated below. This is how
I picture the impact of constraints on your creativity:

By looking at this simple curve we can observe:

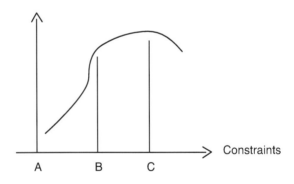

Creativity Stimulation

Constraints

A   B   C

• From point A to B, the more constraints and limitations you have, the more precise your goal becomes and the easier it will be for you to create new solutions. Therefore, constraints can have an exponential impact at the beginning. In this initial phase, just after you receive an assignment or decide a theme to work on, you are excited to jump in and are full of ideas.

• From point B to C, you clearly have less creative stimulation. You may have found solutions to problems or new ideas but have set too many limitations and constraints. It becomes hard to think of all of them and still find something original that works. However, it doesn't stop being interesting at that point. It's worth it to keep digging and to think hard on your problem using the creativity tools I've supplied. Be patient; there are still new ideas to find before point C.

Actually, the path between point B and C might be where you find a great solution or have a breakthrough...or begin feeling like you're at a dead end. Most likely, you are not at a dead end, but it feels like it. As you approach point C, your creative stimulation begins to drop.

• After point C, you set yourself too many limitations and constraints. Whether it is actually impossible to do what you want, or whether you lack the necessary tools or experience to solve your dilemma, you are in a counter-productive area. It is time to let go of some of the constraints and limitations to give some "air" to your brain, some space to create and give freedom to your thoughts.

The annoying thing (that I can't really help you with) is that being aware that you have too many constraints only comes with experience. This is the reason you need to try and fail. Each time you try, you will learn something about yourself; you'll notice how stimulated you become under various constraints, and you'll learn when it really is time to let it go.

Same Problems, Different Questions

So, what now? You understand that you are a genie and that problems and failures are a blessing. You know you need a weapon to fight those monstrous problems and become remarkable. Here is the key: New and original questions kill old problems.

Most people want to get different answers or better solutions to the same problems by asking themselves the same old questions. This could work, but it is likely you'll end up with the same solutions. Now get this: It really, really isn't hard to ask original questions.

If I were to ask you to create ten original questions now, you could do it easily. Actually, you may already know it is important to do this, but you've forgotten. It's easier to go with the flow. So, make the effort to remember to ask further and go beyond; your uniqueness and inner genie will do the rest.

Let's say you have to create a new tablet for your company. You may be thinking, "Can I finish it on time? How can we make it lighter?" You may think about other tablets on the market and consider why they are remarkable. You may identify one or several of those trends.

Now, what different questions can you ask yourself about the creation of your idea? What if you ask yourself, "How can I make my tablet different from the competitor's products? What do people really need when they are looking to buy a tablet? Is making it faster or lighter a priority?"

Take the competition's way of thinking and use it as «a springboard to think differently. Ask original questions to explore original directions! It is that simple. If kids can do it, you can do it too!

When you see someone at the newsstand purchasing a poorly written, low-quality newspaper in the morning, ask yourself what a higher quality journal might look like. Maybe there could be a new blog or a fresh newsletter that you could create.

This type of thinking means you must question everything. With this inquisitive mentality, you question the "normality" of everything you see. This is one of our favourite things to do as magicians. When people consider an everyday habit as "normal," we magicians see an opportunity to fool and mystify them. But let's not lie to ourselves— we humans like comfort; we like the things we know about. When we were kids, we wanted the same bed-time story every night because it was familiar. We never told our parents, "Wait! Surprise me tonight with a story I don't know."

But now, you can surprise yourself with this simple tool. Every day, exercise your questioning muscle. Before you know it, people will ask you, "Wow, how do you get all those ideas?!"

So here is an assignment (I love saying that, I feel like I'm a wise teacher): each day, create ten different questions for one problem you are facing. Look at a problem, consider what people would normally ask themselves about it, but ask yourself original questions. The questions don't have to be great. They don't even have to be good. They just have to be.

Still Stuck? Do the Opposite.

"Do the opposite! Now!"
                            - Ira Seidenstein Clown Master and Teacher -

At some point in the creative process, you'll think you are stuck—but you aren't. But then one day you might be stuck for real. This isn't fun. When you don't know how to continue, you may decide to stop. You may surrender to it thinking, "It wasn't such a good idea after all." It feels like you've wasted time, physical and emotional energy, and maybe even money. However, there is a way that allows you to have a breakthrough before you regret wasting any time or energy. Here is what to do: the opposite.

What does that mean? Well, it means a million things, and that is what is so great about this tool. It is a cheating tool (my favorite kind of tool) to find out new directions without having to think too much (which won't help you get unstuck)! Whenever you do the opposite of what you were doing, you find a new way to approach the same problem. Chances are, you were stuck because you weren't trying to go in a different direction.

So, how do you do it? If you are pushing, pull. If you are pulling, jump. That might not be the *real* opposite, but it might be for you in the moment. Just try new things by doing what is the opposite for you in the moment.

I have been told that the correct word in English is "contrary." There could be several directions that are contrary to where you are but only one opposite. The reason why I use the word opposite is that it doesn't give you much of a choice of where to go. You pick one direction and go there 100%. It doesn't matter if it is the wrong opposite or the right contrary. Just go for it.

Let's say you are trying to make more of a profit by reducing costs in your business (this is often the case). Do the opposite— spend more. Seems stupid? Maybe, but if you dig deeper into such solutions, it might lead you to even more interesting ones, such as spending your money in a smarter way. Perhaps you could learn to invest it more efficiently. The costs are not the problem but the solution.

Are you trying to answer all the e-mails by starting early in the morning? Maybe you should start answering them at noon or in the evening. The book, *Never Check E-mail in the Morning* by Julie Morgenstern, teaches us that, when you reply to e-mails first thing in the morning, "you have on average two to three replies per e-mail." So, not checking them saves you from spending all your precious time answering e-mails. This is another example of having wonderful results with the opposite way of thinking.

Doing the opposite brings you counter-intuitive solutions that you would have never found by thinking hard— and it is more fun!

Nutshell Recap

- We constantly create obstacles in our mind.
  They are illusions.

- You think you need a safety net, but creativity is unlimited
  when you embrace the unknown and give yourself room
  to explore.

- Failure is an invented concept: You can only learn
  through the process of unexpected results and mistakes.
  Nothing bad can happen.

- Every creator throughout history has been rejected— it is
  normal. Rationalize rejection by remembering it is only
one
  idea getting rejected. You can have thousands of ideas
  a day.

- Problem-solving is part of creativity and you can do it in
  a fun way!

- Constraints stimulate your creativity even if it seems like
  a paradox.

- Constraints offer opportunity— until they don't.
  Be aware of this subtle shifting point.

- Ask yourself different questions to get different answers.

- If you are stuck, do the opposite of what you were doing.
  This opens unlimited doors.

Secret #4
Use Crazytivity

Magician's Reveal

A magician's JOB is to embrace the impossible, the absurd, and the "stupidity" of his ideas. Without a little CrAzY in our creativity, and a lot of it in our dreams, no illusions would get created, and no one would come to our boring magic shows. So, we go crazy. Wait... isn't that what kids do? Of course it is, but I think you have heard enough about that already.

However, we magicians go even further: We use our experience and knowledge along with that crazy attitude without letting it overcome our craziness. That is what Crazytivity is all about.

So now, my creative magicians, I'm happy to finally give you the tools I've been promising you throughout the book so far. They will help you to truly access your natural creativity and unleash your inner genie. These techniques will turn you into ninjas of freethinking, the Bruce Lees of creativity. I couldn't offer these techniques early in the book because I wanted you to understand the basic philosophy of magician's (in a broad term) creativity. Now that you are *initiated*, you can learn these practical tools to jump into action.

First, we learned how to approach creativity. Then we, learned how to connect and balance your knowledge with your child-like spirit, and how to overcome obstacles and fears. Next, we go into the heart of this book: the Crazytivity brainstorming method. "Realistic" and "practical" people reading this book, beware! This Crazytivity thing might change the way you see creativity in a magical way.

I can't wait for you to discover it!

"They called me 'Crazy Jack,' and I think crazy is good. We are crazy, but we are not stupid. We know what we do."
- Jack Ma, Founder of Ali Baba -

Act Like Nothing is Impossible

"The most important thing in life is to stop saying 'I wish', and start saying 'I will.' Consider nothing impossible, then treat possibilities as probabilities."

- David Copperfield, Master Magician -

The more things you create (art, business, experiences, or illusions), the more you realize that you can do it even better the next time. We, magicians, know this. We know that even if something is said to be impossible, there is a way to make it possible— or at least, there's a way to give you the illusion it is.

Let's say a client calls me and asks, "I was wondering if you could get our manager to appear on stage?"

I may have absolutely no idea whatsoever how to do it, but still I'll say, "yes, of course."

I know I'll discover how later.

I have a magician friend that received a request to make a building vanish in China (true story)! He did it! and you know what? When we actually do the thing that was believed to be impossible, we often think, "That wasn't so hard after all!" (However, maybe not about making a building vanish).

If you apply this positive attitude towards art or magic, it extends into your creativity, your profession, and your life in general. Whatever you want to create, it is possible. You can create a company, a painting, or a magic show; it is all possible.

Now, I am going to contradict myself and say that some things really are impossible. However, 99%* of things are not. You have to draw the limitations of what is possible even farther than you normally imagine.

Let's say you aim for the stars only to land on the moon. Worst case scenario, you take that huge leap and end up in your backyard. If you aim for your backyard, you'll never land on the moon. Get it? It is a cosmonaut metaphor.

For example, if I were asked to transform you into a frog

*Statistic drawn from an imaginative study in my head. Got a problem with that?

and then back into a human in five seconds, you would say it is impossible and you will be right. I don't think anyone has discovered a way to do this just yet. But if I were to try, I might discover a great way to create the illusion that I can transform you into someone or something else. Okay, maybe not a frog, and maybe not in five seconds but who cares? I discovered something.

Train yourself to shoot for the stars by assuming nothing is impossible. This is the best mental exercise: to imagine the impossible and access your Crazytivity. Just for fun, make a list of all the things you would learn if you tried (with all your passion and willpower) to build a rocket, or to become president, or to build a multibillion-dollar empire, or to become a world surf-champion.

Very Difficult is Not Impossible

"Many things are improbable, only a few are impossible."
- Elon Musk -

Many people assume that when something is very difficult, it is impossible. Many people don't want to put in the effort to work through something tough or complex. Often, they instantly label a task as impossible because it feels tricky. This negative way of thinking often appears way too early in the creative process, and this is usually when we give up. We may even label a task impossible before brainstorming or considering an alternative.

We, magicians, have the opposite strategy. When we hear something that sounds COMPLETELY IMPOSSIBLE, we refuse to believe it is. We think, "There has to be a way! I'm sure it is not impossible." And we work on it by inventing crazy, wild, and out of the box solutions. We do this by using the very tools you'll be equipped with soon! Sometimes our attempts work, sometimes they don't. But even then, we open our mind; we're always ready to find solutions to any problem that is *said* to be impossible. This is a winning strategy because we don't lose time or effort. If we don't get the result we were hoping for, we can discover something else. If we haven't discovered anything, at least we've exercised our minds to build the impossible.

An example of something very difficult I achieved (that everyone else thought would be impossible) was this: I became a magician. When I told my mother I wanted to drop out of college and become a magician, she laughed. She truly believed that I was joking. My father, who was a research scientist his whole life, frowned. I think he was trying to search for a solution he couldn't find. At this moment, I told myself it was going to be really hard. But I didn't tell myself to forget it or that it was impossible.

However, for months after I made this choice, people would tell me my vision was impossible. I'd show them basic card tricks and make mistakes with my shaking hands.

Where would he possibly perform magic? How could he find clients? Do people even want to see magic tricks?

Magic wasn't even popular in France when I started out. But I didn't care. I had a vision, and I wanted to follow it. I just needed to know how; I knew I could learn how.

So, what is really possible, complex, very difficult or impossible? It is for you to decide! But instead of starting off by saying, "Oh, this is just too crazy. I will never be able to do that," do the opposite! Assume it is possible!

Could you build rockets like Elon Musk and spend a couple of days in space? It's possible. That guy did it. It is very hard. You'll need finances, engineering skills, management skills and courage but it is possible. Could you time travel? It sounds crazy and has never been done before, but you could illustrate the illusion of going back in time. Perhaps time-travel is a metaphor. Maybe there is a way, a different way— your way.

In the end, you must always have a positive attitude toward what you can create in your life. You must make it a habit: believing that everything is possible.

This is what I want you to do: Make a list of twenty things in your life that you assumed, or that others led you to believe, were impossible. Look at each item on your list; think hard and be honest. Now write either "very difficult" or "impossible" next to each item. You will be surprised.

Don't Judge Your Ideas

"Good ideas come from bad ideas, but only if there are enough of them."

- Seth Godin -

I don't know you, but I'm 100% sure you are a murderer. You murder poor, little ideas and impulses with no mercy. This must change because the number one mistake people make in art, in business, and life in general, is that they judge their own ideas way too soon. Even if they allow themselves to dream for a while, they instantly want to get back to reality and begin to label their ideas. This is a mistake.

You should continue to explore absurd, or even impossible, ideas for a while longer. Give each idea a chance; they may contain specks of gold you don't necessarily see at first sight. As I've said before, each idea can be used as a trampoline to jump off and then land on another amazing idea. If you judge the idea too soon, you'll never know where it can take you.

Value each idea you have. Only then will it be possible to stop and survey every option in your collection, and then you may begin to connect the dots. Quantity is not a problem— it's quite the opposite. This barrier of self-criticism can be built in your mind without you even realizing it. You may have ten ideas, then go and eliminate nine of them because you think they are stupid or won't work. However, there is a reason you thought of those ideas, as stupid and useless as they may seem. They may not be your strongest ideas, but they deserve to be acknowledged. Don't kill them before they are born! If you really don't believe in them, put them aside for a moment. Let them grow a bit in their own time.

You may say to yourself, "Someday, I'll have a bad-ass idea."

Then, what? Every day you have thousands of bad-ass ideas, you just don't acknowledge them. Don't wait for "someday!" Pay attention to each of your thoughts, impulses, and observations— capture them!

Even if this seems completely weird, treat your next idea like it's the best idea you've ever had. Come back to it a few days later. You may notice the idea has grown, and now you can see the gold in it after all.

If you want to share your thoughts with the Crazytivity Community, come find the Facebook club at: "The Crazytivity Club" @crazytivityclub.

Crazy Solutions For Impossible Problems

"If people aren't calling you crazy, you aren't thinking big enough."

- Richard Branson -

We, magicians, are always facing this problem: The logical possibilities and classic solutions aren't an option when trying to achieve something said to be impossible. If so, it would have been done before. If we want to give the illusion of achieving the impossible, it has to be done in a way so original and unique that the secret to the trick will not be easily discovered.

In other words, magicians try to find alternative solutions to an impossible problem. We do this by going for all kinds of ideas, especially the crazy types. We know that those impossible, stupid, and terrible solutions will lead us to new ideas.

In thinking of how to make a coin vanish, a crazy solution could be to simply put it in my pocket right in front of the audience. Stupid? For sure. Crazy? Yep. But it is a starting point. So now, we have a new problem: how to make this maneuver invisible. Do I redirect the attention of the audience? How can I do this when the participant is always looking at my hands? I don't know yet, but I don't care because I'm only a few steps into the problem-solving process. And if I find several more crazy ideas, I suddenly have several possible solutions.

I could tell a joke at just the right moment and, when people laugh, I could slide it smoothly and casually into my pocket (this is actually what I do in my show, and no one notices.) If I immediately tried to solve the problem of the vanishing coin with the "perfect" solution, I would have hit the wall of impossibility at full speed. I would have given up, just like many people often do. When you have several possible solutions, you can put your experience, and knowledge into practice to actually go through it. The first step is truly this: Generate as many leads as possible without thinking of the viability of each.

For most of you non-magicians reading this book, chances are, you don't want more problems by creating stupid solutions. This may be why you seek direct and conventional solutions; you want to avoid problems. This is the right decision to make, but not when the problem seems impossible. Instead, magicians are used to creating more problems. Therefore, we break the main problem down and find various solutions.

Degrees of Impossibility

Trying to solve something difficult with a weak solution only creates more obstacles and more problems. Stupid magicians… When people try this theory out and see their problems evolve in this way, they're usually ready to surrender to the impossible and stop the process looking at all those problems! But if you do what magicians do, you are actually getting closer to your goal when you think you are getting further. You simply pass degrees of "impossiblity." You went from "it is impossible to fly" to "it is impossible to hide the cables." So, each stupid or crazy solution you find will actually make you think of something valuable.

As I've said before, nothing is impossible. Whatever dilemma you are in, the more you create crazy solutions (that may make your dilemma seem even crazier!), the closer you get to solving that impossible problem.

I know this concept is not easy to understand, so here is an exercise I give in my corporate creativity workshops. I ask the participants to brainstorm on the problem: I want to fly. I have them start the sentence with, "Flying is impossible, unless_____." Each time, the participants reach another "degree of impossibility" and get closer to a solution. Here is an example:

It is impossible to fly, unless_____.

• **1st degree of impossibility:** I want to fly.
-Natural response: It is impossible to fly because we don't have superpowers or wings.
- Unless we had wings.

• **2nd degree impossibility:** I need wings.
-Natural response: This is impossible, we don't have wings.
-Unless we built something such as artificial wings.

• **3rd degree of impossibility:** I need to build wings.
-Natural response: It is impossible, I don't know how to do it.
-Unless I ask someone to build them for me.

We continue until we find a solution. In fact, you are about to try this out yourself with the exercise on the next page!

The "It's impossible ... unless" Exercise

This exercise consists of two simple parts:

1) Solve the "I want to fly" problem with the same structure I've presented on the previous page.

2) Pick a personal problem or project (something seemingly impossible), and multiply the degrees of impossibility by using the same exercise.

Here are the steps for you to follow:

A) Write down a project or dream that seems impossible.
B) Beneath the problem, you will write: "It is impossible because… " and complete the statement with your first response, such as, "because I don't have superpowers."
C) Beneath this statement, write "unless… " Here you will invent a terrific, or silly, or even an impossible solution. You can (and I advise you to do so) invent many of those "unless" responses at each step.
D) You will now respond to your "unless" solution by writing: "It is impossible because… "
Once again, respond with the first answer that comes to you.
E) Continue creating new leads by writing "unless… " Then suggest stupid, crazy, or possibly viable solutions.

At any moment, you can start over with a different lead or crazy idea. Generate as many problems and solutions as you're able. Remember to embrace the impossible; let yourself glide, step by step, from "stupid and crazy" to "entirely possible." Have fun playing with the unknown.

Here are a couple of themes for this exercise you can choose from:

"I'd like to win Roland Garros - I want the world to be a happy place - I want to travel to the sun - I want to eat a cloud - I want to have superpowers - I want to be CEO of my company."

What the Hell is That Box?

Policeman: Tell us what's in the box right now!
Barney Stinson: I can't. Magician's Code.
                    - From TV show How I Met Your Mother -

Crazytivity is not only about problem-solving. It is also about thinking differently. We've all heard the advice, "Think outside the box! Be different; be original."
Hearing this suggestion too many times can be paralysing.
"I should think outside the box? Great! Thanks! I didn't realize that."
Here's the thing: Just because it's been said many times doesn't mean it's some abstract concept only guys like Steve Jobs can handle. Everyone can learn how to do it and can practice thinking "outside the box."

The "box" is actually a metaphor that symbolizes what you consider to be your own limitations. For some of you, this might be obvious. However, remembering this helps us to see the mistakes we are often making: going for the obvious ideas, solutions, and mundane ways of thinking or doing. Because people are social beings, we are more influenced than we would like to admit (me especially)! We go for the most common ways of thinking about something. When we don't, we get trapped in our own head along with our own limitations, beliefs, and habits.

First things first: Get out of that damn box. But how? You've already learned different ways to free yourself from yourself, but you've not exactly freed yourself from your box. This box also symbolizes common ways of thinking; it represents all of the everyday influences you're subjected to. Using Magician's Crazytivity will help you out, big time.

Magicians have to go against mainstream ideas and solutions if we want to create our own magical effects. We have to think outside the box because if we don't, we invent methods that won't fool our audience or participants. That fact they could have thought of that, or that they could connect the dots and figure it out is the risk. They could laugh in our face saying, "I know how you did it!"

Let's say I'm sitting at a large table which I've forbidden the audience to go behind. If I try to convince them I can make objects disappear, chances are, they'll think the objects have been hidden behind the table. It is that simple. Therefore, we need to get out of the box by thinking differently than others. Magicians study their audience's reactions and, over time, we begin to identify patterns. Once we can see them, we try to invent crazy solutions that differ from thinking patterns the average audience member may have. This is also part of the Crazitivity mindset.

Pause and Reflect

Do you know what is going on? What are the people around you doing and why? Are you one of them?

Most of the time, we do the things we do simply because it is habitual. And like Einstein said, "if you always do what you always did, you will always get what you always got."

Here is a visual way of looking at this statement: Imagine that the main way of thinking is like the current of a river, and you are one of the fish flowing with it. It is convenient and practical to go the same direction. But what if you asked yourself, "Why?" What if you turned to swim the other direction to see where it leads?

When you go against the mainstream, people may think you are crazy. They may wonder why you ask yourself existential questions; they may wonder why you can't be "normal".

Aaaaagh…normal. Normal is Crazytivity's worst enemy. Let me tell you something: Do not care what anyone else thinks. Only consider other people's thoughts if you're working to identify the norm and thinking about going against it.

Magicians don't care about what everyone else is doing. We constantly look at the world through a magical lens. We search for crazy and original solutions, illusions, and tricks. When people are going one way, we are thinking of how to go the other way just to fool them. An audience is like a school of fish to us (with all due respect to you guys, of course). To check yourself, follow Mark Twain's advice: "When you find yourself on the side of the majority, it is time to pause and reflect." I encourage you to study your colleagues' common behaviors and habits and then identify common patterns. Here's how:

The "Identify the Box" Exercise

What is interesting about Mark Twain's quote is that he starts his sentence with "when." *When* you find yourself on the side of the majority. He didn't start the sentence with "If." My point is this: I believe we are always on the side of some majority. However, you always have the potential to be more original, more off-beat and crazier. But should you? Well, that is another subject (though I think yes— it's always more fun to be).

If you think this quote does not concern you, well, sorry but it does. You can be a magician, painter, or a modern artist, and you can still be on the side of the majority. Just like other painters, you paint on a canvas with a brush. Or, perhaps you decide to be original, and you paint with your hands. Well, lots of painters use their hands to paint.

I'm not trying to make you feel bad about yourself by saying you will never be original. I'm actually saying quite the opposite. You can always be original by knowing what questions to ask yourself and by recognizing behaviors and habits that other people share. Try this: ask yourself questions about people like you. Study people in your profession, in your country, in your same creative field. Study your family, your friends and people in social situations. The aim is to identify what is going on by taking a step back. Pick a group and ask yourself:

-What favorite books do they have in common?
-What common thoughts do they have on various subjects?
-What shared attitudes do they have toward life and work?
-What hobbies do they have in common?
-How pessimistic are they about certain subjects?

This is an everyday exercise you can do. Notice everything; identify patterns. Make mental notes or write a list.

When you analyze and question your observations, you will train your brain to see what patterns we all adopt in some form. After identifying them, it will be very easy to escape these patterns and create something original or "out of the box."

The CRAZYTIVITY Brainstorming Technique

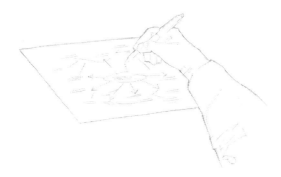

Yes! You have made it! This might be the most important part of the book as we combine everything we've learned so far into a super powerful technique. This technique allowed me to sell my ideas professionally as a magician. Nothing compares to this brainstorming exercise.

A company once came to me with the strange request to create a show using vegetable oil. I said "*sure, no problem,*" and asked for a couple of brochures and information about their product. Boy, that was a long brainstorming session. I knew, however, that all I needed was a pen, paper, and the Crazytivity brainstorming technique.

I ended up revamping an old cups and ball routine by using olives and some cups made of vegetable oil. At the end of the routine, tiny bottles of olive oil appeared beneath the cups. I also decided to juggle with eggs from grass-fed chicken, and I invented a trick using lipstick produced. I created a prediction game: I had the audience envision nature with a landscape, and I created the illusion of grains disappearing and reappearing.

I had fun. And all I needed was my brainstorming method, a pen, and paper. I know you can invent crazy things too, whatever your job may be. So, let's start with the basics.

The Basics of Brainstorming

Imagine a wild and crazy storm. Take a few seconds to visualize what this storm would look like in your neighborhood. Imagine what it would look like. Imagine all the things that would go flying in the air: the roofs of houses; cars lifting and swirling past. Now imagine that the wind and lightning represent different ideas. This is a good interpretation of the word "brainstorm". A brain...storm.

And I know this isn't what Alex F. Osborn -who popularized this word, meant by "Brainstorming"; He meant to use the word "Storming" as a metaphor for a military assault (in a specific context: a squad of creative people exchanging ideas). But I like the image of a real storm better, because I believe it underlines the necessity to go for a quantity of ideas in a fast and (maybe seemingly chaotic) way. If we try to be too careful or too smart too soon (as in a...military assault), there is a risk that we censor ourselves, even more so when we brainstorm alone.

With this technique, you will learn to create volumes of solutions as fast as possible in a visual way. The quality of the ideas you generate doesn't matter. They can be stupid, crazy, absurd, or pretty good. You just have to move fast— and crazily.

The idea is to generate ideas so quickly that your rational mind won't have time to judge them. After a few minutes of this fast-paced exploration, we will stop and allow ourselves to look at the amazing things we've discovered.

A Combination of Two Techniques

As I began experimenting with this type of brainstorming, I realized I was creating a mix of two techniques: mind-mapping and freewriting. Mind-mapping is simply writing one word or a concept in the middle of a piece of paper. This word is usually written in a circle or a square. You then come up with words that relate to the central subject and connect them with surrounding circles. This exercise allows you to visually display what is on your mind, and it helps you make connections easier. But the main thing that improves results when brainstorming is being carefree and moving quickly in the first steps. When I read the great book, *Accidental Genius*, by Mark Levy, I understood that my Crazytivity technique is also similar to the freewriting technique. Freewriting consists of writing as quickly as possible without caring what ideas come out of the session. In his book, Levy advises his readers to use a time constraint to force them to write even more quickly, in addition to other awesome suggestions. This made perfect sense to me as I looked for ways to improve my brainstorming method.

So here you have it: The combination of freewriting and mind-mapping equals the Crazytivity Brainstorming Method!

Let's Try it Out!

Step 1: Throw it Out There

Before I order you to jump into the unknown, try out this method using an example. Let's say I want to go into outer space for a couple of days. Here's how I'd illustrate my brainstorming process using the mind-mapping technique:

This is what I discovered in just three minutes. Can you see how I bounce to a new idea when one single word reminds me of something? I arrived at the idea "advert bean" because the word cosmonaut reminded me of a funny commercial that Heinz company had on television. Going to space makes me think of the word levitate, and then I asked myself, "Do I really need to go into space to do that?" So I wrote, "What for?" I will remember this lead and dig into it a bit later. I also thought I may need extensive training to explore space, so "I wrote long studies." This expedition will cost money, so I wrote, "pay for it."

One idea leads me to so many others. For this first step, you don't need to find "real ideas" that are ready to be used in the real world.

The Time Constraint

With this exercise, it's important to set a timer for three or four minutes. This time constraint will help you go as quickly as you can. So now, it is your turn. Take a piece of paper and a pen and write a word (or a couple of words) that describe the theme you want to explore. Draw a circle around your theme. Then, as quickly as you can, write all the words, ideas, sentences, elements that quickly come to your mind. Don't drop your pen to think, just write it all down, even if it doesn't make sense. Are you ready? Throw it all out! GO!

- - - - -

All done? Congrats! You have completed the first step! (For those who didn't, get back to work! You have to try it out and play along to understand the dynamic of this exercise... If this is the first time you've tried this kind of exercise, it's pretty likely you had trouble stopping to think too much. It may have been difficult to keep your pen moving and to write continuously. This is normal. And don't worry, you'll have many other four-minute sessions in your life in which you can try and perfect this counter-intuitive habit. The key is to get everything out of your subconscious mind without a filter. Just lay it all on the table.

Step 2

Once you complete this first four-minute session, put down your pen and notice the amazing things you've found. You may be ready to cast out some of the ideas you came up with. Before you do, check each idea, one by one, to see if there is something to take from it. Think and reflect for a few minutes.

For example, in the "a couple of days into space" exercise, I realized I should decide WHY I want to go to space first. Is it for the sensation? For the view? What price (in terms of money and time) I'm willing to pay to go there. So that is what I'll brainstorm next and that lead me to other simpler solutions. If I really want to go up there, I might be having to travel for a government institution or maybe with a private enterprise like Space X. I could be taking this trip because I'm training to become a cosmonaut, or maybe I'm a passenger along for the ride. Maybe I'm a crazy guy, like the guy who jumped from space with a parachute and a Go Pro on his suit. Well, I don't want to spend time studying to become a cosmonaut, so I will go with one of the other ideas. I'll dig deeper on that.

It doesn't matter if the balance between interesting ideas and ridiculous ideas is 10% versus 90%. What matters is that you now have the foundation for yet another brainstorming session from ideas that you quickly threw out there.

My next brainstorming session will be about why I'm going into space. Am I going for the excitement? For the view? For the challenge? To fulfill a childhood dream? From here, I'll start Step 1 all over again.

On a new sheet of paper, I will write, "Why I am going to space?" I will circle it, set my timer, and brainstorm like a madman all over again. And later, if I feel like I need to explore something else, like "spaceship," I'll write it on a new blank sheet, set my timer, and explore that.

You can repeat this first step as many times as you'd like using a new element of the brainstorming results. Personally, I like to go crazy and do it at least five times with ideas I found during the "throw it out there session." I prefer to really explore the subject.

Step 3

Step three begins when your timer is ringing to finalize step two. Now it is time to connect some dots. Everything we've discussed in this book so far converges to this very technique: making connections. First, liberate yourself, stop thinking, and then create a volume of ideas. Now, stop and look at what you've got. Try to find as many connections as you can between seemingly unrelated elements by using connection tools we've learned, and by simply letting your mind wander. If you find an interesting connection between two elements, this may be the subject of a new brainstorming session.

Step 4

The fourth and final step is to let it rest. Once you think there is nothing more to find, it doesn't mean it is the end— it is quite the opposite. However, your conscious and unconscious mind needs a bit of time to digest all of this new information.

I'm super lazy; I usually stop after two or three brainstorming sessions and take a break. If I started brainstorming in the morning, I might start again after lunch. I may try once more before bedtime. And I don't do this only because I'm lazy…I do it because it helps me to work unconsciously on the news leads and ideas that I've discovered. You might be surprised at the solutions you can create if you sleep on it. Another way to look at it is to pretend to drop it, to let it go and then *boom* you come back to it by surprise! That works especially well with problem-solving!

Whenever you feel ready, come back to your work with a fresh look. You'll have new ideas to discover new paths.

That's it! This is the only brainstorming method I use and is my favorite one. This doesn't mean you can't explore different brainstorming methods. You can even modify this one into something that suits you better! The most important thing is to generate a VOLUME of ideas using a time constraint and lack of judgment. This technique can be done solo or with a group of people. It can be done on paper or verbally. The most important thing is to practice and to have fun!

Create the Impossible With Pen and Paper

I started using this technique when I began creating custom magic shows for companies. I've worked for Colgate, Rogé Cavaillès, Terre Oléo Pro, and many others. I am not a logical, think-hard-to-get-the-best-idea-ever kind of guy. I naturally go with the craziest ideas first then narrow down my possibilities.

Before I knew anything about mind-mapping, before reading any books about creativity, I used this brainstorming method. I guess what I'm trying to say here is that I'm a f****** genius. Okay, I may just be saying that creativity is natural and that everyone can do it.

I am able to answer unrealistic demands from clients immediately, though I let them think I've worked for weeks. I just need a pen and paper to open the gates of Crazytivity. The real work is having the capacity to move beyond mental blocks and to train your creative muscles; the real work is invisible, and it is hard. It is like magic: If you have good presentation skills and a few sleights of hand, you can entertain the world with a deck of cards. You don't need a huge budget, an office, or the latest technologies. You only need your Crazytivity.

I usually start my brainstorming sessions with the question, "Wouldn't it be cool if ___ ?" That is how I created a show for the Colgate company in which I used a toothbrush as a magic wand. I've developed custom ideas for improbable products such as nose spray, deodorant, and even coffee using this technique. This invaluable technique can really be used for improving anything: business strategies, marketing, life goals, personal problems, and much more.

If you are a manager, a team leader, an entrepreneur, or CEO, I have designed a special article for each chapter. To access them, simply go to my blog at this address: www.butzisblog.com

Nutshell Recap

- Crazytivity is about using impossible, stupid, and crazy solutions to solve problems.

- Always be aware that what seems difficult is not really impossible.

- Deciding anything is possible is a mental trick to help you shoot for the stars.

- Never judge an idea before giving it a chance; it may contain gold.

- Multiplying degrees of impossibility is the best way to get closer to a viable solution.

- Don't be afraid to base your thinking on stupid ideas to solve impossible problems.

- If someone says something is impossible, add "unless..." and see where it leads you.

- Pause and identify the box. Then give yourself the luxury to think differently by asking yourself different questions.

- Brainstorm like a mad man (or woman) by creating many ideas and connections.

Secret #5
Connect the Dots

Magician's Reveal

Creativity is all around us. Every object, every concept, every thought, and every event can be a source of creativity. Inventors and creative magicians know this. They know that the world is like a playground and that any element is waiting to be connected to a project, an illusion, or a fun presentation. They know creativity is all about connections. This might seem abstract, but this is the perspective of the creative mind. Steve Jobs once said:

`Creativity is just connecting things. When you ask creative people how they did something, they feel a little guilty because they didn't really do it, they just saw something. It seemed obvious to them after a while. That's because they were able to connect experiences they've had and synthesize new things.'`

Think about it:

You connect your visions with your craft.
You connect your dreams with your reality.
You connect skills with other skills.
You connect talents with other talents.
You connect ideas and concepts with each other.
You connect your personality with your knowledge.

Acknowledge any element as a source of creativity, and let it manifest by connecting it to another element. Once you know this (and you do know this because I just told you), creativity becomes very easy, and the results look like magic. Magicians continually connect objects to each other and with other elements, like rabbits and a hat. We connect gimmicks with magical effects to achieve our visions. We connect old methods with new technologies to keep the audience freshly fooled— and we are no smarter than you.

In this next section, I will help you learn to make your own connections. I will give you very powerful and simple tools that your inner genie will love.

Serendipity
[sɛrənˈdɪpɪtɪ]

noun

The faculty of making fortunate discoveries by accident.

Serendipity, for me, is a type of connection. It is connecting what just *comes* to you with your current projects. It often supplies the missing piece you were looking for. I used serendipity to create my very first magic trick.

I love this concept because it reflects how unpredictable life can be and, at the same time, it reminds us that we can do something about it. It is where the concepts of exploration and connection meet. By looking at the definition, you could think serendipity is just being lucky. However, there's more to it. Approaching serendipity as a creator means adopting a specific state of mind toward our creative process. It is accepting the exploration process and following whatever comes. And the more you follow what is happening to you, the more things will happen to you.

Some think serendipity comes from a spiritual source, others think it is just a bunch of coincidences. Some believe it is luck, others believe it is a very rational process that can be explained. Whatever you chose to believe or not believe, serendipity is there. It is happening to you, and if you chose to do something about it, it will lead you to amazing discoveries. It is the easiest way to make connections; just go with the flow, and follow everything you notice. Take one single thought and play with it to see where it leads you. Explore, and let the connections be.

Serendipity is How I Invented My First Trick

A while ago, I was working on the ending of a card routine. I wanted to use another magician's ideas of having a signed card appear within a remote control, but I felt like I should find something different and not copy someone else's idea. I couldn't find anything new and, after a while, I let it go.

During Easter, I went with my family on a trip to my aunt's house in the country side. The kids were hiding chocolate eggs (with toys hidden inside) around the house and the garden. I thought, "I want some chocolate too. There was absolutely no reason I couldn't have a chocolate egg with a toy." And so, I took one— a big chocolate egg that I opened into halves. Inside was a little stuffed animal. I instantly thought: "Wouldn't it be awesome if it had the signed card inside?!" It happened to have the perfect specificities I was looking for to achieve my illusion. What a great coincidence! To be honest, I didn't care if it was a coincidence or not, I just went for it as the connection happened in my mind.

Combining Objects

Magicians love objects. We get inspired by their specificity and the story they hold. We love to combine objects with various methods we know to produce original effects. Sometimes it is unconscious, sometimes we actively think of new ways to use them. We create lists of objects that inspire us and connect them with an effect or gimmick. We see a pack of gum and imagine how it could be transformed. Better than making unconscious connections, doing it consciously trains our brain to be inventive and to create them.

So, for you to understand that creativity and great innovations are all about connecting dots, I thought of a very simple adaptation of this active state of mind: We will simply connect two objects with one another. This is a great exercise to understand the principle of connection, and it's also a great exercise to develop your connection skills.

Combine a shoe with a stick, and you have stilts; combine a board and some wheels, and you have a skateboard. Of course, the examples are not always straightforward. You can find unlimited combinations by brainstorming a few minutes on combining any objects.

So, here is a little exercise for you to play with this concept. You see the list of words on the next page? Since you are reading on your Kindle or e-reader, recopy them on a sheet of paper (half of them is enough). In a second, you will close your eyes and link two words randomly with a pencil. When you open your eyes again, pick one connection, take a pen and paper and imagine all the ideas that could be created by combining those two words for three minutes.

When I do this exercise in my workshops, participants always have amazing ideas, crazy possibilities, and out of the box revelations. I'm sure you will too! Ready to experience that? Well...go!

Gum	Keys
Smartphone	Wallet
iPad	USB stick
Coffee	Chapstick
Tea	Bracelet
Pen	Cake
Sweater	Book
Watch	Glasses
Shoes	Bottle
Coins	Plastic bag
Table	Glass
Visa Card	Knife
White sheet	Balloon
Window	Earing
Ear phones	Spoon
Headset	Coaster
Cap	Christmas decoration
Scissors	Stuffed animal
Trombone	Bike
Business card	Plant
Lamp	Newspaper

How did it work for you? Pretty funny exercise huh? Look at how many ideas you have created with just two words. Imagine if you brainstorm several times with various words, every day. You could generate thousands of ideas! Well, that is what great inventors do every day consciously or not, by just looking around them. And now you can do it too.

Sometimes, the simplest tools are the most efficient, and I strongly believe this is one of them. Always come back to it when you are looking for new ideas. Simply refresh the list of words to new ones that relate to the subject you are working on. Have fun!

Connect Objects to Concepts

"Learn how to see. Realize that everything connects to everything else"

- Leonardo Da Vinci -

Okay, now that you know you can connect objects to each other, the leap to associate objects to concepts and ideas is pretty easy. You may have begun to make these associations in the previous exercise already. It is easy to go from an object like "headphones" to "music." Something material like, a dollar bill, will probably lead you to think of "money," and therefore, "online transfers." This exercise is unlimited if you allow yourself some freedom to extend from objects that are concrete to concepts that aren't physical.

All you need to do is take an object, put the sign "+" beside it, and then write a concept (or whatever comes to mind).

I look around and see a little kid and a flower. If I'm a designer, "kid" + "flower" could make me think of a new line of clothes for little girls. If I'm an artist, I could think about how to accurately paint the relationship between kids and nature. As a magician, it makes me think of making flowers appear for a participant on stage. It is that simple.

Another obvious example: just look at what you have in your pocket: your smartphone. Your phone is probably the biggest combination of ideas, objects, and concepts in existence. It is a phone combined with the concept of mobility. Then, someone thought it would be cool to send messages with it. And from then on, the phone became the container of endless objects and concepts. Now, everyone has music on their smartphone as if the iPods, that were so popular only ten years ago, dissolved themselves into new machines. This is without mentioning the flashlight app (light + phone), MMS (pictures + SMS), taking pictures (camera + phone), the ability to create video (camcorder + phone). And then, of course, the internet (opening the door to connect you + infinite information).

And don't even get me started about the light sabre app (Star Wars + phone). Apart from those obvious features, you can also transfer money, use your calendar, take notes, download movies, Skype and Shazam songs; so many possibilities combined in one device.

An example of how I connected an object with a concept in my own magic is when I used a stethoscope to give the illusion of reading minds. I decided to pretend I would *listen* in the participant's head with an instrument designed to hear someone's heartbeat.

This is a combination that sounds almost too simple to be true but, as always, it doesn't mean it can't be surprisingly efficient. Especially for children. Suddenly, I'm no longer the intelligent adult who reads minds, but *they* are in the spotlight with one end of a stethoscope to their temple.

This idea suddenly opens many more doors for me creatively. I think of even more stories and funny situations to play around with. I envision a whole universe of fodder for the stage by connecting an object to a concept! So here is what you can do: Pick one object around you and explore what happens when you connect it to three different concepts. Then, find three ideas each time. You will be surprised by the results!

Connect Concepts with Other Concepts

"A software is a great combination between artistry and engineering."

- Bill Gates -

I don't even know if I should explain this one. I think you get my point. But I'll continue to spell it out for you, and give you examples to learn from. Once you become aware of the connections you can make between an object and a concept, it's really not hard to start connecting concepts with other concepts. You might actually do it inadvertently! However, being aware of making connections sheds light on what top innovators and artists do unconsciously— and it is a fun game to play.

Let's mix the physical object "mug" with the concept of "productivity." You might think of making coffee, a productive breakfast meeting, or of designing coffee cups with inspirational logos. You might think of a factory that makes "to-go" mugs.

Another way to practice making connections is to start with two objects and find concepts they are hiding. A laptop = internet. A wallet = finance. A building = design. You have thousands of different connections to make.

Once you are aware of these kinds of connections, you will begin to see them everywhere, as our beautiful brains always allow us to do. You won't bother trying to start from scratch but will playfully use connections that are already existing (but only seen from your unique perspective). The more you notice, the more you train your creator's eye, and the easier it will be to create connections for your projects anytime, anywhere.

Let's try this exercise: Pick two random objects, figure out the concepts related to them, and then figure out ten original ways to combine them.

Easy, right? Well, you can do that all the time, whether you're walking down the street or completing a fast creativity brainstorming session. In my opinion, it is best to always go wild, create tons of ideas and leads, look at what you have, and then start focusing on what can be connected. Classifying them and labelling them is not on the agenda for now!

Combining New Technologies and Old Concepts

"Nowadays, people are taking pictures with their phone, right? [...] but then they are just sitting there. So, what if they would take a photo and instantaneously put it on the line? [...] It would be called Exchangeagram."
- Billy McMahon in the movie "The internship" -

Until the day I interviewed Jeff McBride, my magical mentor, I had never thought of it, and yet, it was obvious: Magicians combine old methods with new technologies to create original illusions. The more I thought about it, the easier I understood why magic has taken certain directions in the last few years, such as with the use of iPads to the use of technology as a method to achieve effects. And let me tell you this: Magicians use it all! Bluetooth,

Wi-Fi, smartphones, special magical apps, micro-cameras, vibration receptors for code messages, and a hundred more gadgets and technologies can be used to give an illusion. And with that, we mix many old methods such as sleights of hand, misdirection, fake thumbs, and so on.

I recently created a video of a prediction that is saved on a SD card, with details about it that were just thought by the audience. How? I won't tell you. I have to keep the secret, but it was not very different from classic magic. I used old methods and mixed them with new technologies. The only thing innovative in this illusion is that, instead of using paper folded four times for the prediction, I used SD cards. It isn't a huge improvement, but sometimes you don't need much to make a project original. Any little change or connection can lead you to other connections.

So, what are the new technologies you can apply to old concepts? What new inventions from this lifetime can you connect to ideas that have existed for thousands of years? It isn't as hard as it might sound. You look at a book and then an iPad and BOOM! Kindle. You think about meeting the love of your life while having your phone in your hand? BOOM! Tinder. What about having an assistant? Add "virtual" before the word, and you get one in India for half the price!

A tip: The more you use technologies that just came out (or even better, a technology that is about to come out), the more it looks like magic.

What Lens Are You Looking Through?

If you start noticing the various connections all around you, you can start shifting your mind from noticing to acting, from passive to active. As you do so, you will see plenty of opportunities to make connections around you: from the moment you wake up, to the things you watch before going to bed; from what you encounter at work, to what you see on the internet. What you look for, you will find. Unlimited connections are out there waiting to be seen by you; they are waiting to be applied to your projects, work, and art.

The more specific you are, the easier it becomes to find solutions. You can't *look for creativity* out there. You look for a solution for the problem you have in your last project. Don't wait for permission. You are allowed to do it.

When I first started creating tricks and having ideas, I would Skype my mentors, Jeff McBride or Larry Hass, and say, "Hey, I had this idea but I'm not sure if I should do it..." They would always reply, "Sure it sounds fun, do it!"

After a few times, I realized I was just asking for permission to try it out and they'd always give it to me. The irony struck me: I can give the permission to myself. I don't need to Skype for that. You just need to know what it is that you are trying to connect, have one end of the thread, and it becomes easy to find something around you to connect it to.

A lot of magicians claim that they are looking at the world through a magic lens. I can really identify with that. Whatever we see or hear, we instantly think of how we can connect it to a routine, a trick, a sleight of hand, or even an object, prop, or gimmick. I bet you look at the world through your own type of lens too!

So, what is your lens? What do you have in mind most of the time? What is your main focus? Within what frame do you want to create? Is it art? Is it a new business idea? Mine is magic: everything I see, whether it's performance, visual art, or random posts on Facebook, I think of how to link it to a routine. So, what is yours? You may even have a couple of lenses as you are changing your focus from time to time (no pun intended). Although it is harder to see everything through two lenses, you can change frames regularly (pun intended) by changing lenses or by refocusing. The most important thing is your attitude. A deliberate change of focus doesn't need to be energy consuming. You don't have to think all the time. Just be ready to make connections in a fun and light mood. In my online course, I even go out into the streets to show you how easy it is. Actually, I want to give you two exercises...

Practical Tools to Connect in the Real World

Tool #1 – The Inspiring Object

There is nothing magicians like more than getting inspired by an object. I see a vintage hourglass at a shop and think, "Oooh, that is a cool object. I could totally use it to do a trick about time. Maybe the card vanishes slowly as the sand moves through the hourglass until it completely disappears and... " I go on and on. My wife just rolls her eyes and hopes the hourglass is not too expensive because she knows I'm "off with the fairies," like my clown teacher used to say. And it turns out, I'm not the only one. Many magicians have a thing for inspiring objects that create the spark they were looking for to start a new fire.

My question is: Why can't you do the same? You don't need to be a magician! And I don't want you to become an impulsive buyer either! I don't buy everything that inspires me as objects I already own can sometimes be inspiring. Just use physical objects that you like, love, or find interesting as a starting point. Then let your mind wander to connect it to a story, a project you are working on at work, or a song you are writing. Just have an attitude of being open to what is around you.

Perhaps you see a chair in a shop and suddenly have a business idea. Why not? One chair could inspire the business model for a shop— what you will design, the upholsteries you may use, or whatever you're inspired to see. Follow it; don't block it! Write the idea down and give it a chance to see where it leads you. Even if your idea appears to be impossible, it might connect to something else and lead you to another idea. Go to a mall, an antique shop, a toy store, or a souvenir shop, and let your mind wander. Look through your lens; see what those objects might bring you.

Tool#2- The Opportunities Game

If you can figure this out, you can do it with other various concepts. How? Complete the same exercise but instead of making connections with objects, try making connections with businesses, random situations in life, or social interactions you observe. This is a way to open your mind to what is happening everywhere and to help you make connections with what you care about. Try this when walking down the street, or strolling through a mall, or in ANY SITUATION. Look around you and let yourself become inspired by any element, asking yourself, "Why not use that for my current project?"

Let's say you are an employee of a company. Let's say the lens you are looking through is a marketing lens; a commercial operation you are working on requires you to find new ways to attract clients. You see a cool car driving by with loud music blasting. Maybe you could use this idea? Maybe you don't like the car, but you think about the music. You think having a good band play at a launch event might be good advertising. Maybe there could be a raffle for someone to win a car. Maybe you decide you don't like this idea at all, but you stay open.

Next, you see someone working on a Mac computer. Though there is really nothing special about this scene, if you are willing to really look for opportunities through a lens, you can create something. This person might be a good intern to help manage some elements of this very operation. Maybe a Mac computer makes you think of an iPad; you then think of a cool digital interactive game your future clients and current clients could play to learn more about the company.

It actually doesn't matter! The exercise is to help you *extract* opportunities out of normal, everyday scenes of your life, and therefore, your imagination leads you to connect it to other existing elements.

Imagine you're looking through a business lens, and you see a

guy slapped in the face by a girl. You don't know why it happened, or what he did, and frankly, you don't care. You are just looking for a business opportunity. But what does this scene make
you think of? There is always something to connect it to, especially if what you see appeals to you. Maybe guys don't know
how to pick up girls— you think of a dating coaching business
or maybe a dating app. Maybe you think this girl could have
been in danger; therefore, you conceive an alert whistle for girls
in danger.

I don't know, I'm inventing as I'm writing, and frankly it doesn't
matter if the ideas are good or not. We've learned by now that
an idea will always connect with something else: a better idea,
an already existing business model, a color, an event, or a design.

About Those Tools

These tools are great practice. They help you open your mind to
make more creative connections with your world unconsciously
and consciously. At first, it may feel a bit weird. Personally, I had to
force myself into thinking, *What around me inspires me?*
But, with time, it becomes easier and easier. And you don't need
to be a genius to do it. So, good luck!

**Hey you! Yes, you reading! Don't forget to share some of your stupid
ideas on The Crazytivity Club on Facebook:**
facebook.com/crazytivityclub !

If you are a manager, a team leader, an entrepreneur, or CEO, I have designed
a special article for each chapter. To access them, simply go to my blog at this
address: www.butzisblog.com

Nutshell Recap

- Creativity is not about being smart or intelligent.
  It is about connecting the dots.

- Your life and the way the universe unfolds is serendipitous.
  Go with the flow to connect the universe with your mind.

- Connecting two objects can open a thousand doors to
  new ideas.

- You can connect any object to any concept to create an
  original idea.

- Connect two concepts to get something original.

- Old concepts will always be there. New technologies will
  always appear. Connect them both, and you will get
  something unique.

- Decide what lens you want to see life through;
  the connections are waiting to be made.

- Provoke chance by grabbing opportunities to actively
  connect with your environment.

Secret #6
Change Habits
to Cultivate Creativity

Magician's Reveal

Every good life coach will tell you that you can only begin to change your life once you change your habits. So, when people ask creative artists and entrepreneurs, "How did you think of all that?" they are asking the wrong question. They should ask, "What are your daily habits that make you more creative?"

Tim Ferris discussed this very concept on his podcast *The Tim Ferris Show*. Adopting the right daily habits, and being active in the creative process, is what will have your creative brain ready to go. If you don't do anything, nothing happens. You want to wait for the greatest idea of all times? Great, let's wait.

Did you wait? Nothing happened, right? Yep, it is normal. Magicians actively look for inspiration. We actively incorporate the right reflexes and attitudes so that we can build on ideas, make connections, and invent fun illusions.

I wish people didn't always ask the question, "How did you do that?" They'd learn so much more by asking, "What does it take to create something like that?" They should ask, "What do you do every day to create new illusions?"

They would learn more by asking these questions because I never reveal a secret just to reveal it. I reveal something when I know people are motivated to actually learn it, whether it is a magic trick or a creativity tip I can provide. The craziest thing about this is that most habits you need to be creative are not secrets! There is no magical formula kept by some ancient dude with a long beard living on the top of a mountain that will make you more creative (that would be awesome though).

Habits are the secrets in plain sight that you are looking for. Habits are the single most important thing you can change in your life to change your identity. Incorporate the right attitude with these habits and get amazing results.

By simply altering our daily habits, we become more creative, invent greater illusions, and build moments that we think are magical. Our habits help us create the impossible. You can do that in your own life too. So here are a couple of super simple habits that I believe you should incorporate into your daily life to better cultivate your creativity.

Fake it Until You ~~Make~~ Create it

"You must be the person you have never had the courage to be. Gradually, you will discover that you are that person, but until you can see this clearly, you must pretend and invent."
- Paulo Coelho -

Our brain needs time to adjust to change; especially when it comes to changing habits. This is also true for creativity. Our brain won't believe us immediately if we tell it that we are suddenly creative people— that a magician has told you to trust your inner genie and it will begin sending us ideas every day. We need to show our brain (technically, ourselves) that we can do it. But how?

Hopefully, you can *fake it until you make it.* This is the first habit: the habit of faking it by adopting creative habits. This means you don't need to wait to get it all to start creating. That is the best way to never start. The best way is to embrace the impostor syndrome, and start pretending you are Da Vinci or some other kind of genius.

Why? Because you will start changing your habits, even if you don't believe in them at first. What would you do if you were Da Vinci? How would you act every day? You would draw, look for opportunities to create new inventions, paint, study, and more. I doubt that Da Vinci would stay in front of the TV, then have coffee with a friend, and then come back home after a party at 2 am, complaining that he isn't creative.

Look at the habits of any innovator or artists you admire, and see that their habits are key. You will learn there are periods of time during which each of these creators work at specific things. If you were to imitate these people you admire for a month, the way you look at things will change, along with your skills, creative habits, and insights.

Do you know why people don't fake habits? It is because they think creativity is a given gift or that some have a natural talent while others don't. I also believe this is true. Like I said before, we are all magical potentially. But I also believe we all need to develop that potential.

When you first start out, don't be scared if nothing happens. Most of the ideas I used to have when I first tried to create magic were written in notepads that I threw away. They were, for the most part, unusable and bad— but it doesn't matter. I was faking it and, soon enough, the ideas I had were becoming better and better because I was training my brain to think like the best.

Changing habits takes time and patience and is a long-term strategy. This is why most people don't do it. They don't see the results NOW. But faking habits is a daily training. And it is NOT hard. Actually, here is how…

Write it Down

This is the key to trusting your inner genie: Write down every single one of your ideas. I write everything down. I take notes on my phone in the movies when I love some camera movement or lighting used (and people think I'm addicted to my phone). I write in my notepad at the museum when I realize what the artist must have felt. Even in the streets or in the subway, when I suddenly think of a tiny improvement on my show or keynote speech, I write it down. I record ideas on my phone or will even send myself an email.

Why? Because it is a commitment. I'm telling my brain and my inner genie, "Look, I trust you, bro! I'm writing it down."

In my eyes, this is the first step to feeling creative. Once you have a notepad full of ideas, you can't feel uncreative or say that you are not creative. You can't say there is not an inner genie inside of you, and this will start to change your identity a little bit.

You'll go from, "No, I'm not really a creative guy" to "I'm not super creative, but I have some ideas." Soon you'll be thinking, "Yeah, I'm pretty creative."

This changes the game. If you believe in your inner genie, you get the number one thing you need to become more creative: confidence. Capturing ideas is a way to concretize concepts that were previously only conceptual. It is bringing your dreamy states to reality and your imaginative gems to maturity. It is one step further in the creative process, and it is easy to do.

However, it is also easy not to do, as Jeff Olson mentions in his book, *The Slight Edge*. This is always the case with little reflexes and habits that may not yet be habitual.

So, take note of this little habit: Write down every stupid little idea to begin trusting yourself more, bit by bit, idea after idea.

This requires an investment of three dollars for a pen and notepad, or zero if you like having your ideas on your phone. If nine out of ten ideas are very, very bad or ridiculous, don't worry. This is normal. Just keep in mind that one might be interesting and lead you to other good ones.

Woody Allen was famous for writing each idea he had on a piece of a napkin or the back of a receipt and collecting them all in a drawer. He'd write down anything: a line a character would say, a piece of the plot, or a fun ending for a movie. Later, he would come back to that drawer and choose one idea to develop.

A Virtuous Creative Circle

"If the theory promoted creativity, then all teachers would have been the inventors."

- Soichiro Honda -

A study showed that the difference between creative people and non-creative people is that the more creative ones thought they were creative. That's it. Dozens of participants were asked to generate ideas and find original solutions throughout a series of tests and they were then interviewed. The only difference between the most creative group and the other one was their level of confidence in their creative potential. They simply believed they were creative. That simple. In order to create that belief in yourself, gradually change your habits and attitude to create a synergy, and change your identity from "I am not creative" to "yes, I am creative."

This synergy is like a virtuous creative circle and can be achieved by incorporating the simple habits we have seen in this book. It is also a psychological, self-fulfilling prophecy at work.

Here is how it works: You think you can create something, so you start doing it. You find an idea or two and think, "Yes I am a bit creative."

So, you open up your mind a little more and make new connections in your environment. Next thing you know, you have two more ideas (and better ones)! As you are working on them, you think, "Man, I am creative."

Because you think you are creative, you unleash the inner genie a bit more. You look around for more opportunities to create in original ways, and you will find them. You will have another idea, and you will write it down. And now you can think, "Wow! I write down my ideas! I am creative!"

This goes on and on until you become unstoppable. Even if you are taking baby steps at the beginning, they will slowly become giant steps with synergy and time. Trust your inner genie and decide to follow this upward spiral for amazing results!

The Virtuous Creative Circle

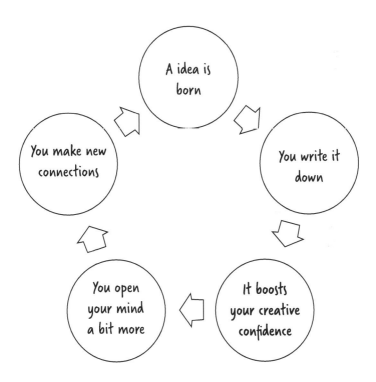

Take Voices and Visions Seriously

"An artist is not paid for his labor but for his vision."
- James Whistler -

Have you ever had a little voice in your head trying to guide you through the noise, giving you a solution to a problem or even just suggesting something? Have you ever closed your eyes to see yourself doing something without knowing where the vision came from? Have you ever seen an object and then visualized yourself using it in an original way? I'm sure you did because we all have those visions and voices in our head. And this is a type of magical moment as well.

However, what we often love to do is shut these visions down; we tell ourselves it was just our imagination playing tricks on us. And you would be right to believe that! But what would Da Vinci do? Would he say, "Ah, it is not worth it"? No!

Magicians and creators decide to pursue those clues, wherever they come from. We take our visions and inner voices very seriously. Let's say the vision is horribly shitty. Well, we try to see if there is something we can do with it, and if we don't, we still write it down somewhere. Sometimes it is a dream that comes to us in a visual way, like envisioning ourselves making an audience laugh. Sometimes it is just a small idea, concept, or improvement on something we already do, such as a new twist on a card trick. It may be a song stuck in our head that makes us think, "Yes! That's it! I want this song for my act!"

Do you feel stupid following those visions and voices? Do you feel like an impostor? Welcome to the club! When it feels too right or even makes you feel guilty because it was so easy, this is usually when you've found what you should do.

I love to go to movies for this reason; I'm in awe when I see the masterpieces directors produce by following their visions. Some film and photography directors are masters at this. They see a scene in their mind and move heaven and earth to make it come true by using movement, colors, lighting, actors, and amazing scenery. They trust their inner genie to bring their visions into reality, just like magicians. And you, what can you do with your visions? Do you take them seriously?

Follow Your Intuition

"Your intuition opens doors to opportunity that your logical brain will never even notice. So... trust and follow it."
                                                    - Sonia Choquette -

Intuition is the most efficient way of making connections, and you already have it. A common belief is that we don't have *enough* of it. But you have to listen to intuition to develop it. Like imagination, you can't quantify it, but it is a huge and necessary tool. Intuition is all of your knowledge connected somehow in your subconscious where you have stored everything over the years. Since we can't really explain where intuition comes from, some of us might think it comes from a higher power. But whether it is the god you believe in, or simply the power of the human brain, it doesn't really matter. It is here, it is part of you, and it is an amazing tool for creativity and other areas of your life.

So, how can you listen to your intuition? There might be a voice in your head on top of which you are trying to think. There might be an uncomfortable feeling you are trying to ignore or that you are simply ignoring unconsciously. You can rationalize all you want; it is still there and won't disappear until you address it. You need to listen to it and acknowledge it. Don't worry if it is hard to hear; our intellectual brain is always trying to prevent us from doing stupid things anyway. You won't jump off a cliff because you think that you should, but the intellectual brain is so present that it hides and distorts all signs in your body. Have you ever noticed that it mostly happens in your gut? Your brain sometimes thinks it knows, but your gut actually does know.

Science has shown you have grey cells in your stomach. Think about that. My friend Sonia Choquette is a master at teaching how to listen to your intuition. You should check out her work if you want to go further in depth on that subject.

Some subconscious connections won't appear as clearly as others (like clear visions, ideas, and solutions), but they'll give you a hint— a clue that must be heard. You can ignore these clues and only rely on your rational brain; this might actually work for you. But whether you like it or not, wherever you think it is coming from, you will miss out on potentially amazing connections if you keep shutting down your intuition.

Great artists have great intuitions, and they pay close attention to them. So, when you feel something a bit weird, or think you hear another "you" talking in your head, listen to it. Don't let the rational mind intervene in the conversation. Try to follow it to see where it leads you. Your inner genie, the authentic "you," is trying to talk to you. Ignoring him is a like slap in the face.

The Little Story of How I Almost Missed Creating My First Illusion

If I had chosen not to go on the trip to the countryside during which I used a stuffed animal to create the magic trick "Ginette," I might have never created anything. If I didn't have that stuffed animal, I may have found a different crappy toy that didn't inspire me. If I had been working on another piece of magic, I may not have had the right connection in my mind to inspire my vision.

In France, we have the proverb, "With 'if's,' you put Paris in a bottle,' meaning, you can't change the past by saying, "If this or that happened…then…" You can only use what you have in the present and look forward doing something about it.

With that said, let whatever comes to you (a phone call, a message, a billboard, or the way a leaf falls from the sky) be an opportunity to connect dots and create a vision in your mind. Follow your gut, intuition, and little voices. You don't know where they come from? We don't care. It is there. Use it. It doesn't matter why it comes to you, why you believe it comes to you, or what would have happened if you would have done something differently.

My story would have had a horrible outcome if I didn't follow the vision I had with that stuffed animal and if I did not write down my idea.

Creative <u>First</u>

"Amateurs sit and wait for inspiration, the rest of us just get up and go to work."

- Stephen King -

Now that you know creating feels damn amazing, that it sets you apart from others, and that it is the key to generating value in your life, you don't want to get caught in a reactive state. You don't want your life outside of creating to take over by always answering e-mails and phone calls and not having time to develop your creativity.

The best habit you can take is to prioritize your creative time instead of your reactive time. Otherwise, your agenda is always going to be about fulfilling other people's agenda and not about producing your own work. You won't be expressing yourself. You won't be creating value from your uniqueness. You won't set yourself apart. You'll just be helping others do so.

What is really important to you? For me, what's most important is the happiness I achieve through the value of the work I create. Therefore, in addition to helping others, I can more effectively contribute what I have to offer to the world. I can't achieve this type of happiness if I don't put creativity first. I can't live any other way. If you don't prioritize creativity in your daily schedule, you will end up like 90% of people. You'll become wound up in a storm of "things to do" that other people have decided for you. Your creativity dies at this very moment. And then you die. Ok, I went too far again.

This means you have to be able to say "no" on a regular basis. You have to be able to realize what your priorities are, and you must recognize what others try to make you think is more important. It also means you must learn to organize your schedule in a way that you feel helps you create the most. Protect this time BEFORE answering your plumber about his quote or responding to your colleague about his power point presentation.

Try this on a daily basis: Wake up and create. Don't wait for the storm. Plan sessions of answering e-mails throughout the day, so you don't break your flow when working on your projects.

Check out Tim Ferris's *The Four Hour Workweek*, for amazing advice similar to these suggestions. And ask yourself, "What is really urgent? What is really important? Can he wait one hour?" (I can tell you, the answer is usually yes.)

Can you shut down your phone for 20 minutes to do three crazy brainstorming sessions? (I bet the answer is also yes.)

It is worth it to create time for your creativity. If you are overworked, go on a quest of improving your productivity and efficiency at work so you can create that time. All great minds, like Chopin, Thomas Mann, or Matisse, protected their creative time. So can you.

Treat Ideas Like Plants

If the ground is your mind, seeds are the information, ideas, connections, and feelings you bring to the soil

Watering is the equivalent of your conscious thoughts and reflexions

Different plants you grow represent the different kinds of ideas you can have

Discovering solutions means your plants are blossoming

I love this metaphor because it helps us understand we don't necessarily need to think hard to create ideas. Developing your thoughts is as necessary to creating as watering plants is necessary for them to develop, live, and grow. However, at some point, you have to take some distance and let them grow by themselves. If you give them too much water, they will drown.

The same can happen in our creative process. Your brain works all of the time, and when you take a break from working on an idea because you're feeling stuck or overwhelmed, you often find the solution. You know what I'm talking about: magical moments. Those are moments where your plants grow by themselves. So, you need to give some space to your brain to process your thinking and make new connections unconsciously, exactly like you need to let your garden enjoy the sun and digest the water.

This is why every time a client gives me a theme on which I have to create illusions, I consciously give the idea to my brain to work on it, and I do something else completely unrelated. When I come back to actively work on the problem, my brain has already found a couple of solutions, passively.

Some people experience this as the last piece of the puzzle. They work on a problem for so long that, after they relax, clear their mind, and let ideas grow by themselves, the final piece of the puzzle comes to them. How fortunate! This is not a coincidence; it is the result of your unconscious thoughts, baby.

Experienced creators and problem solvers know how to play with this tension-relaxation balance. They will think hard, *let it rest* (though I prefer to say let it grow), and come back to it later. You can experiment with this as well, and you'll get better over time.

Take something you are working on and apply this technique: work hard, let it grow and come back to it again. Become the gardener of your mind.

You can apply this approach to being creative with or without a deadline, with or without a client. Find a seed, water it a bit every day, and let it grow. Do this all over again with dozens of seeds. After a couple of months, you have a beautiful garden and your life has completely changed.

Surround Yourself with Dreamers and Doers

"Seek out people who are willing to level with you, and when you find them, hold them close."

-Ed Catmull, Founder of Pixar,
President of Walt Disney Animation Studios-

If you decide to surround yourself with an entourage of skeptical, realistic, and pragmatic people after this chapter, I'll have to officially expel you from the Crazytivity religion. Seriously, I think it is a mistake to not take this habit. It took me a looooong time to understand this habit and put it into practice: the habit of having exciting, fun, and creative people around you.

I will tell you something: there was a time when I was a little depressed about magic. "How can this have happened?! Magic is amazing, it is your passion, you should love it..."
These responses I kept hearing didn't help. My mentor, Jeff McBride, told me, "It's because magic feels like a job to you now." He was right. There was no creativity involved, no excitement to find something new anymore. I had to trigger it. He told me to hang out with more artists, magicians, jugglers, and fun people to get inspiration. I thought, "Really, that is your advice?"
But now, years later, I realize he was right. At the time, I was living at my parents' place, and though they were wonderful to me by supporting my art despite my unconventional path, they weren't quite excited by the same projects I had and didn't motivate me much. Actually, they were kind of worried.

Often, your family and closest friends want to protect you. Therefore, they will tell you not to "dream too much", so you won't be disappointed. They think you will waste time, hope, and maybe even money. That's sweet, but you don't need protection for Crazytivity— you need craziness.

Of course, you can't just stop seeing these people— they are your friends and family. But you can identify the pessimists; you can identify who worries compared to who is encouraging, and then you can decide who to listen to.

In moving forward, find people who inspire you to invent and to attempt crazy ideas, and spend more time with them!

There are plenty of dreamers and doers out there: artists, entre-preneurs, travellers, explorers, miracle workers, ukulele songwri-ters, actors, sword swallowers, and a thousand of other kinds of "-ers." There are plenty of awesome people who dare to follow their dreams. Meet them. Whatever job or passion you have, there are cool people out there who can stimulate you, and chances are, they are feeling lonely too! They may be painting alone in their apartment or working alone on their Mac in a coffee shop (oops, that's me) wishing they could have a coffee break with someone like The Rock, or Tim Ferris (yep, still me).

So, take on this habit: find "people of your kind", as my friend David Brower says (he is one of them, check him out). If you look for the most supportive people, you will find them. And when you do, their dreams, enthusiasm, craziness, and inventive boldness will be contagious. You'll catch that awesome disease they have, and you will love it.

Your "Work" Environment

Some say that whatever environment you work in, if you are crea-tive person, you'll be creative. Some others say that your envi-ronment directly influences your creative state. My point of view is this: You need to find your own balance. You need to take the habits from your work environment that stimulate your creativity and maximize them to the highest level. A lot of creative people feel that a work environment should be so comfortable and fun that it makes you feel like you are not working. Even though some of you may approach creativity in a more serious way, you can find inspiring factors that resemble your definition of enjoyable and fun. This type of environment helps you more easily reach a state of flow and become more efficient.

"Flow" is when time flies, and you are incredibly productive. It is when you start working, and then, five hours later, you stand up thinking it has been only an hour. This often happens to creative people when their work environment is just right.

For some of you, this environment may consist of having a thousand toys and stuffed animals on your desk to nurture your inner child, like some of the designers at Pixar. For others, it might be a minimalistic and sparsely designed environment. For another, the perfect writing environment may be a room with a view of the sea. With that said, there is no work environment that can be the best for everyone. You have to explore, try out different places and decorations, and observe what works best for you.

Try switching environments during the day, during the week, or even different seasons of the year to see what works the best for you at what time. A good work environment will help you feel fresh and motivated… and it is not a small thing in the creative world. To help discover the environment that is just right for you, experiment with these different factors:

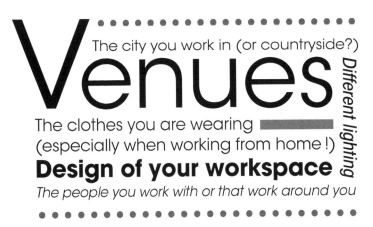

Venues

The city you work in (or countryside?)

Different lighting

The clothes you are wearing
(especially when working from home!)

Design of your workspace

The people you work with or that work around you

With that in mind, you can totally do different kinds of creative work in different kinds of spaces (for example, I like to write in cafés with a lot of light and space, but I don't like to edit my videos there. I love to practice magic at home, but prefer to rehearse my keynotes in a rented space), and be more inspired for each task.

Go to Inspiring Places

"I have found that sitting in a place where you have never sat before can be inspiring."

- Dodie Smith -

As a magician, I love going to shops that sell 1000 different objects: souvenir stores, craft shops, and books stores. If I go to these places with a relaxed and open mind, I know I will find a lot of ideas, whether they are stupid, amazing, or promising. Often, these ideas can be in the form of visions.

For example, I was looking for an idea to publish in a magazine, so I went to Hema. This shop sells everything from lip balm to Christmas chocolate, not to mention kitchen utensils, kids' toys, and thousands of cute things to write letters and notes. As I walked through the aisles, very slowly, trying to digest all of the information gathering in my mind, I found a set of stamps, each one capable of printing a letter. I don't know why or how, but I instantly saw myself placing them in a bag, and then handing them over to an audience member to write out a word I would predict. My brain connected dots unconsciously, and there was no way I would let this idea slip away from me— so, I wrote it down. It turns out, it was a good idea that was later published in a magazine article.

If this can happen to me (and a thousand other artists), you can do it too! If you have a problem at work you are trying to solve, go to an inspiring place you know…or don't know! It could be a museum, a shop, an Apple store, a bridge at sunrise, or wherever inspires you. It can be close, far, inside, outside or related to art or cooking. It doesn't matter. What matters is that this place it is different from the usual. This is a fun way to make the project move forward. And when the vision comes, capture it! It can be a voice, a quote, an image, something you feel like doing, a concept, or an idea that feels stupid… it doesn't matter.

I once had to create an illusion for a magazine addressed to teenage magicians. I had no idea what to do. I needed to find something young, fresh, fun, and easy, but still super-efficient. I decided to go to a video game store,

and I walked around slowly with my pad and pen. I was relaxed but open to anything that would come to me.

I found amazing things in there: figurines, game consoles
that I didn't know about, replicas of famous video game characters, and something called "pop toys" with big heads on a spring.

I felt stupid and old despite my age. I asked the seller
what these pop toys were and if they were trendy. They were trendy, apparently, and I felt even older. But my pad was full of stupid
ideas, and the pop toys were in pole position. I ended up creating an original prediction with pop toys on the theme of and
had so much fun! To get to this point, I followed my intuition and
gave each little idea a chance.

Moving physically is a great way to move mentally.
When we are still, we are often getting stuck in our own thinking
patterns.

If you are stuck, share your ideas and thoughts on The Crazytivity
Club at this on this page: www.facebook.com/crazytivityclub

If you are a manager, a team leader, an entrepreneur, or CEO, I have designed
a special article for each chapter. To access them, simply go to my blog at this
address: www.butzisblog.com

Nutshell Recap

- Act as if you were creative, and you will become creative. Fake it until you become it.

- Write down everything that goes through your head to gain confidence.

- Take your visions and voices seriously— even if they seem stupid.

- Intuition is the most powerful tool you have. All you have to do is listen to it.

- Create first, then react to what comes to you. You might have to learn to say no.

- Give space for your ideas to grow. Don't work hard on it all the time.

- Value small changes. They will add up over time and lead you to huge ones, especially in changing your identity.

- Your work environment, your creative space, is not a necessity but a great stimulation to your creativity. The better you know yourself, the more creative you will be.

- Dreamers and doers will inspire you. They will push you to actually achieve your dreams and to create. Find them and make friends with them.

- Go to inspiring places when you are stuck or want to get some inspiration.

Secret #7
Dare to Create
for the Real World

Magician's Reveal

Magicians are a rare species. On the scope of creativity, we are somewhere half-way between an abstract painter and a businessman. We have the freedom to create amazing things, but we are also limited. We create to perform and to actually show something to an audience. And even more, it has to "work." It has to fool our audience, to make them laugh, and to make them dream. We need to be bold to try it out; it takes bravery to bring our babies into this scary jungle. Of course, we are not the only ones who have to be brave, but many components of our career require action and courage.

When I began having my first ideas for magic, I would fill pages and pages in my notepad. While travelling in Mexico with a friend I met on the road, he said to me, "Wow, you are writing a lot of ideas! Are all magicians like that?"
My ego loved it. I thought, "Damn, it is true. I'm creative."
I answered him, "I don't think so," with flattered humility.
But looking back, I don't remember what I did with those ideas. I just remember trying one or two of them and getting discouraged. I threw the notepads away. What actually made a real difference is when I decided to act on my ideas. When you get to this point, it makes you an innovator. And this is your last step.

By now, I believe this book has given you the tools to build, nurture, develop, and produce amazing inventions, solutions, and pieces of art. However, your attitude toward creativity in the real world is crucial.

"Daring ideas are like chessmen moved forward.
They may be beaten, but they may start a winning game.'"
- Johann Wolfgang von Goethe -

The Difference Between Talkers and You

"Be a doer, not a don'ter."
                              - Jonny Wu, in the movie "No Pain, No Gain" -

Have you ever met someone who told you that he could have invented the iPod (or any other great invention)? Has anyone ever told you that he has many ideas but no time to work on them? That these are great ideas, but they are waiting for the perfect time to actually do something about them?

These people are talkers. They looooooooove to talk. They talk about how they could have done this and that. They talk about how it is not hard to create what you have created and then give you advice on how to do it.

But what have they done? Nothing. Zero. Can you feel through my words how much these people piss me off? There is a reason for that. It is because they put down dreamers and actual creators so that they can hide their lack of confidence.

You are not one of those people. I know this because you picked up this book, purchased it, and you've read up until this point. This shows great effort on your part; it shows you have the right intentions for the future. That is the first element: the intention to act. But there is still a trap you can fall into that I want to help you avoid. It is the trap of not doing anything with any of your ideas.

Unless you are selling your ideas, and that is your actual job (which is rare), you have to do something with what you create. Bring your talent into the real world. If you don't, your ideas are pointless; they will always exist as a conceptual *maybe*, and you'll never learn the true lessons of experimenting.

So, consciously decide to do something with them. Of course, some of them will be impossible to bring into the world, and that is okay. But shifting your brain to act on all of them will help you do something with some of them.

An idea will always stay an idea and have no impact if you do nothing with it. But remember, one idea can change the world, even just a little bit. I can change your world. Just one of your ideas can bring improvement to your life, can be a solution to a problem, or bring you to knit a pair of wool gloves so your kid will have warm hands. All of this starts with the intention of acting on one your ideas, and continues with the courage to actually do it.

Don't be a talker. Be a real creator. Act as if you want to make Einstein proud.

Be Bold and Take the First Steps

"The important thing in life is not to be a champion. It is to have balls. "

- Julien Boussuge- MMA fighter -

Thinking that your thoughts are good enough to be shared with the world takes audacity. To act on your ideas, you need to be bold. I didn't want to tell you this earlier because this informa-tion can feel scary and paralyzing, "Be bold, be foolish, and be amazing." When you don't know if it is possible, it could have the opposite effect. Now you know.

But the thing is, knowing is not enough. Don't be one of those people who nod with their eyes closed when you tell them about your latest discovery as if it was self-evident. They think they know, but they don't. They don't know from experience. They haven't tried it because it requires too much audacity to take action!

People are going to reject your ideas. They are going to laugh at them and be angry before they accept them. You have to be bold to hold on to them. This is why I emphasize the impor-tance of building your self-confidence! Not only will you have to stand against the wind, but you must continue to walk against it. Everyone is afraid. It is okay to admit it. But, you have to take action against that fear.

I always feel this way the first time I perform a new trick. I remember when I first performed my trick that uses M&M's. In this trick, people think of a celebrity as I eat the candy. When I show them the rest of the M&M's in the pack, the face of the celebrity they envisioned is printed on each of them.

Sounds like a great trick, but when it is time to show it, my hands are shaking a little bit. Will they like it? Is it good enough?

It turns out, people love this trick. And if they don't, does it really matter? Not if you know you are bold enough!

The more courage you have to shift your brain into "bold mode," the easier it will be. Think about an experience in which you were initially reluctant, and then you actually went through with it: jumping from a bridge, rock climbing, whatever rollercoaster you were brave enough to ride.

It often follows the same pattern. You say, "No way. No way."

Then, somehow, someone convinces you, and you then shift to, "Ah, damn it, I'll do it" mode.

You go for it. It scares the shit out of you. When it is over, adrenaline rushes through your veins and you want to do it again. The next few times you try, it's never as hard as the first time. It's like a child's first experience with swimming. It is a nightmare for them to go into the water at first. Then, they gain confidence and want to stay in the water forever, jumping around and splashing you when you are trying to read in *tranquilo*. It is the same with creativity. So, get your courage, and take the first steps!

From Paper to the Real World

Being bold when you are creative has one purpose: to turn your ideas into action. But how? In my opinion, the best way to make this happen is to follow this succession of events:

Get ideas – capture them – develop them – do something with them.

The only stage we haven't discussed is how to get from developing them on paper to actually doing something with them. There is a reason why: You have to find out how yourself. What works for me won't necessarily work for you. That being said, there is a common trap that I can prevent you from falling into: becoming a passive creative thinker.

You have thousands of ideas, but they are somewhere in a notepad. Your smartphone or tablet is full of notes that are sleeping, waiting to be used. You feel good, you feel creative, but others think you are a talker. This is fine if you are already using some of your plans, but it is a real problem if you are not.

Your ideas are screaming, "Use me! Please use me! I'm viable, put me into the real world!" and you can't hear them! I know good creators that fall into this trap. What a waste!

Here is my suggestion: You need to develop a "just in time" system, with as minimal stock as possible (to give a business analogy). The more ideas you will stock in your notepad, computer, or phone, the less likely you will be to actually read them and do something with them.

Personally, I write down my ideas in different types of notepads, and I regularly consult them. When I do, I decide what their destiny is. I go through my ideas and notes and tell myself, "This one is for my new magic show I'll work on in July," and I put a note in my schedule. "This one is for my book so it is on my today's to-do list," and I put it on my to-do list. "This one is for my business but it isn't the priority, so I'll put it down on the agenda and take action on it next month…let's say Thursday the 13th at 8am, I'll start the day with this". "This one is just a thought but I love it, I'll store it with those other thoughts in this folder

I make conscious, small efforts to do this regularly. You can easily forget to do this, or you may think it is unimportant, but next thing you know, you have 50 ideas stored everywhere.

You'll begin thinking, "Ugh, I have so many ideas. I should probably do something with them one day," but you won't. It is so much better to follow through on just one idea than to have one hundred sleeping in your tablet.

Make the effort to "empty the trash can" (if this way of describing it can help you). This process is super easy if you do it every few days or weeks. However, it will become impossible if you do it every month.

My advice is to organize your ideas, and then schedule designated times to go through them before you have too many to manage. Make a decision with each of them. If you don't want to use 20 of them, great. Decide to throw some away, but don't let them get stuck in a notepad full of promising ideas. Organizing it this way will help you take the first steps. These first steps are no longer a scary concept but something to do in your agenda. Write your ideas wherever you want, that is none of my business, but regularly re-organize them into your schedule. Be bold enough to do something with them.

Small Changes, Big Impact

"It has been said that something as small as the flutter of a butterfly wing can ultimately cause a typhoon halfway around the world."

- The Chaos Theory -

This might be the single most important advice I can give you on creativity in the real world: Don't expect to have big ideas right away. Instead, trust your little ideas, and expand them until they have a huge impact. Why? How?

First of all, expecting big ideas is the best way to block yourself. However, following little ideas to achieve small changes will encourage you to take regular action. It will help you change the way you look at your environment and at how you can act in it. All of those small improvements will compound over time and help you gain confidence in your creative spirit. You'll begin to see the changes you triggered in this world. Don't try to invent a cure for cancer or create the new iPod right away; just notice the simple, daily things you want to improve.

You may want to change the way co-workers on your team communicate with their manager. You may want to address a problem with a tool or software you use and work on how it could be more efficient. You could think to organize after-work drinks to bring your colleagues together, or even buy a rose for the receptionist who is depressed and overlooked in her job. Any creative solution, strategy, or gesture you can bring is a small improvement that will have an impact. If you do one small change a day, you will have seven by the end of the week. It is important to realize that any small idea will:

-Shape your brain to take action on your visions
-Have a positive impact on someone
-Help you gain confidence in your creative abilities

When you have enough confidence and actually walk your talk, you can aim higher and higher, until it is ridiculous. Small changes can always lead to crazy ideas anyway.

So, find three little things you can change at work, at home, and in your environment, and decide to create a solution for them. Find simple things to do just to open your awareness a bit more. Take the time, every day, and over a few weeks, you will see huge results.

Create Urgency and Deadlines

"Give me a date and place, and I will compose a show."
- Ariane Mnouchkine- Founder of "Theatre du Soleil" -

I hate deadlines. Book deadlines, deadlines to send presentations, deadlines for my goals (and many others) because I know I'll have to think hard to reverse engineer my everyday work. And if I don't make the deadline, I'll hate myself for not respecting it. However, there is one kind of deadline that really works for me. Creative deadlines. If I agree to create a magic show with a proposal deadline of May 15th, my mental energy and imagination will fire up.

For a while, I didn't want to believe this pressure worked with me creatively, as it usually doesn't with other things. Years ago, I may have said, "Deadlines? Not for me."

But I now know that time constraint is a powerful creative ally. So, my advice is: Don't be afraid of time constraint! Your brain will sense the urgency and will work twice as hard! (Yes, personifying the brain is my scientific explanation for eveything.)

Actually, now that I think of it, the best ideas I've had were the result of the pressure to meet a deadline; from creating tricks for magazines that were due monthly to creating my TEDx presentation (I was informed about the talk just three weeks prior).

I recently learned that creativity in the human mind is greatly triggered when a sense of urgency is raised. Humans had to get creative when the time came to go out in the woods to find something to eat. Frankly, I think you already knew that.

When we are in our comfort zone, we have no motivation to find new solutions. If a pipe beneath your sink is slowly leaking, you don't care. However, once the pipe explodes, you become MacGyver! You find the tape, glue, and tools, or you call the plumber! Problem solved.

Deadlines and urgency trigger action. Pressure is helpful if you are hesitant or having a hard time taking the first step; it forces you to dig into your willpower and do something with your ideas.

If you can understand the importance of this pressure, you can also see that assigning yourself deadlines can be a powerful tool. Sure, it isn't like having a paid client tell you he needs a show in five days, but it is still something. You can even ask a friend to be accountable for you; this will create the sense of urgency on purpose.

Let's do something. Pick two ideas and write them down on a piece of paper. Then write ten ways to create a deadline for each, whether the time constraint is measured from yourself, or someone else puts on the pressure. Pick one and actually go through it! Your brain will love it and tell you that you are amazing ;-)

Learn to Receive Feedback

"People support a world they help create."

- Dale Cawrnegie -

"I don't want to talk about my idea; I'm afraid someone may steal it." I love when I hear people say this. It makes me gently smile because I think 90% of ideas have already been invented (most of them before Jesus Christ); it's how you bring them into the real world with your uniqueness and specific set of skills that will make them original.

Most ideas are impossible to steal. It is fear that prevents people from sharing them. Many people are afraid to hear what others think. But here is something to bear in mind: People will give you valuable feedback, additional ideas, concerns about your projects or ideas, and they will help you spot your weak points— if you allow them. People want to help you create your dream.

The tricky part is that around 95% of people don't know how to handle feedback, criticism, and advice. If this number (that I have created like most stats in this book) is correct, then I would say around the same percentage would say they can handle it. Even when we are used to receiving feedback, it still hurts to get it in our face.

After my shows, I often ask people if they liked it or what they would change if they were me. I'll ask, "What did you hate? Did any part feel too long?"

Although I'm asking for feedback, their answer always feels like a slap in the face. I nod, take notes and say, "Yes, you are right, totally. That it is a good point, thanks."

But all along, my guts are tightening, and my heart is crying. My stomach is saying, "Duuude, let's get out of here!"

Of course, they are talking about my baby here; they're criticizing the fruits of hours of my labor, my creation— a part of myself. How dare they! Sometimes, you haven't even asked for feedback, and someone tell you what they think. How can people be so cruel?! But wait a minute. Why did they say these things? Oh yeah, right, to help you. Let's not mistake who the enemy is here. Yes, most feedback is horrible; people are harsh and inconsiderate. But we are even worse at receiving it. Our ego is hurt. All we hear is that we are not enough. We are not smart enough, not creative enough, not original enough, and not skillful enough. But guess what? They are not talking about you. They are talking about what you shared with them.

Top magicians, creators, actors, innovators, and entrepreneurs arrived at their levels of success because they learned to use feedback as a springboard. Meeting their critics helped them reach what they've achieved. They'll leave their ego to the side for a moment, nod and say, "Thank you," use what was useful and ignore what wasn't, leaving their ego to the side for a moment.

If you have real trouble receiving feedback, I highly suggest you work on it. I recommend the book: "The Six Pillars of Self-Esteem" by Nathaniel Branden. If you need an additional little push to start working on this challenge, here is one...

The Feedback Game

For the sake of your creative training, let's make it a game, a fun exercise.

Step #1 Pick an idea you have that is not really awesome (yet). Try using an idea that you don't really care about.

Step #2 Choose five random people you are going to present it to. There is no risk here— you don't care about the idea.

Step #3 Imagine that their feedback is like a rose thrown at you: it hurts to catch it, but there is beauty in it. Remember, they've thrown the roses because they support you.

Step #4 Talk about the idea and get as many roses as possible. Catch them, write them down. If it hurts, it is not against you as a person. It is the exercise, the idea. Just nod as if you are super interested and thank them.

Step #5 Go home, put your emotions to the side, kick your ego in the nuts, and write down all the feedback, improvements, and suggestions people have given you.

Step #6 Be honest; aren't there several suggestions that will help you develop your idea? Look at them for what they are, not for what they could mean.

This little exercise helps you begin to deal with feedback and draw the good from the suggestions of others. It helps you extract the useful information and leave the emotion and doubt on the side. You have to use the exercise like a colander; learn to keep what is necessary.

If you can do it with ideas you don't care about, you can start to do it with ideas you do care about. Yes, it is more difficult, but the advice will be even more valuable. Just remember that people are sometimes jealous but, most often, they just want to help you.

Dare to Take 10 Creative Minutes a Day

"Any time you see what looks like a breakthrough, it is always the end result of a long series of little things, done consistently over time."

- Jeff Olson, The Slight Edge -

Creativity takes time. But it doesn't take as much time as you'd think. I would argue that ten minutes a day is more than enough time for you to create amazing ideas. Hiding behind the "lack of time excuse" is ridiculous.

Let's say you try ten minutes a day of creativity gymnastics. This could easily lead you to one or more of these achievements:

-At least fifteen leads on one theme
-Two Crazytivity brainstorming sessions of four minutes each (equals twenty plus ideas)
-The time you need to go through your notes and schedule the development of your ideas
-At least five active connections between various concepts

This seems like a good deal of activity, I know. But the testimonial that I receive most in my Crazytivity workshop is, "It goes really fast. I didn't know I could produce so many ideas in such a short time."

Time constraint forces creativity and your natural potential is revealed. But we don't want to believe in our potential. We don't want to believe that it can be that easy to create new ideas. It is only when we dare to do so that impressive results arise.

The advantage of taking those precious and focused few minutes is that we dare to give a place for creativity in our life. Even if it is only ten minutes, it is already something. Like Jeff Olson says in his book *The Slight Edge* (that I highly, highly, recommend), those daily efforts and little time slots will compound over time. I'd add that they will create a synergy in your identity. More and more ideas will begin to arrive in better quality. The more you sit and do it, the easier it becomes, and the more fun you will have.

Take this time. Dare to tell yourself that you, as a creator, need time to express your thoughts.

Ten minutes is nothing. You can be glued to your Facebook time-line watching cats fight dogs for ten minutes (I've been there, and it was longer than ten minutes). It is the amount of time you waste in front of the TV just trying to find something to watch and not even watching it! The funny part is that, when we commit to taking ten minutes a day, we usually sit for even longer. We don't want to stop. However, if we don't feel like going further, it is okay because the goal was just ten minutes. Counterproductivity is not possible here, so go for it!

Enjoy the Process

"All the lawyers and the business stuff is work, but actually creating stuff isn't work. It's good effort. It's hard work. But, it's not work. It doesn't feel like work because the result is very rewarding. "

- David Copperfield -

What does Copperfield's quote mean? That even if you need to work, creativity helps you enjoy the process. And when you enjoy the process, you:

-Have fun working and creating new possibilities
-Don't see that time flies when you are doing it
-Find new challenges to push yourself through creation
-Enjoy learning new methods to create
-Love to find an original object you can explore with

If you are feeling annoyed about creating, if you feel bored doing a job, if you feel *used* by someone deciding what you should create, or if you feel untrue to yourself for not doing what you think deep down you *should* be doing, then something is wrong.

However, feeling bored or depressed is a great place to be because it means you are at the beginning of a crisis that will make you grow as a creator. You are on the verge of creating something great. Don't ignore it, accept it. Go through these low times by asking yourself questions that may lead to hard truths. Change what you feel you should change.

Creativity is, in the end, a great way to get in touch with what you really want from your life. It helps you to be more resourceful and productive, yes, but it ultimately helps you be more authentic. Don't ignore your feelings, intuitions, or little voices when they tell you something is wrong, or you'll be on the path of imprisoning yourself in a life you don't want. Real creativity allows you to free yourself to live the life you want and to create the change you would like to see in this world. But to accomplish this, you have to dare to be authentic and true to yourself.

If you feel like you need to change the methods you use, the habits you have, the people you hang out with, or the environment you are working in to get closer to your higher life mission, do it. You may simply seek more inspiration or ways to have more fun working on your projects— just make the change. You don't have to do it all at once. Remember, small changes are the key. Constantly micro-adjust simple factors in your life— you don't need to wait for the big crisis! One day, you'll find that sweet spot of enjoying the process; you'll remember your fun, childlike way of being the creative person you are.

My Gift to You

Just so you can have fun and because you have finished the book, I put online a video for you to learn your first card trick. Go at: vimeo.com/**25**4**684**786 and type the password "1stCardTrick" to access this tutorial for free.

On top of that, I know that not knowing how to explore or wander in the unknown can be scary or even annoying. So to help, **I've created a map you can use**. At any time in the process, you can start from the first phase to help make sure you are on the right track. Use it to be sure you haven't forgotten anything along the way.

Where? What?

Try to know where you are going. If you don't, you might not get there! If this is ok with you, then start anywhere and explore! The important is to start ACTING.

Explore many stupid, crazy, and impossible ideas

USE THE CRAZYTIVITY BRAINSTORMING METHOD.
Don't think too much at the beginning— it tenses your brain and blocks all the out of the box ideas.

Connect

Connect all the leads, words, and ideas with your new tools!

Develop

Develop those ideas, make them better, expand them and connect more dots. Then, let it rest and come back to them later!

Select

Keep the golden ideas AND the other ones. They might ne useful later or be gold in another context!

Apply

Fight to get your ideas in the real world.
Don't let them die in your notebook— share them!

Nutshell Recap

- Creativity is what should transform your work into something enjoyable.

- Don't underestimate your ideas and initiatives.
  They WILL change the world, one small impact at the time.

- What is the most important is not to talk about how great your ideas are but to actually do something with them.

- With time and the right habits comes confidence.
  And with confidence comes new awesome creative abilities.

- The best way to become an innovator is to find out a system to go from paper to the real world.

- Creating urgency and deadlines is what will fire up your creativity

- Feedback is a chance. Don't let it pass you by just because of your ego.

- Creativity is what will help you enjoy the process of working.
  So, enjoy the process of creating!

The End...

... And the Beginning of Something New

And… this is the end. Bravo! I'm always impressed when people finish "how-to" books because it usually means they have the intention to actually do something with what they've learned and have created a change within themselves. I hope it is the case for you because if it is only an ephemeral desire to act that is not followed by a real change in your habits and actions, what's the point of reading all this?! Like the philosopher Al-Ghazali said,

"Knowledge without action is wastefulness and action without knowledge is foolishness."

To refresh your memory and help you create a plan of action, let's first recap a little bit what we've seen so far. Now you know that creativity is in you and that you are fully capable of developing it. You know how to free yourself from your limiting beliefs and from situations you are stuck in with childlike fun and imagination. This optimistic attitude will allow you to wonder, aiming higher than you have in the past. It will help you to ask yourself different questions and to go for silly, improbable, or seemingly impossible ideas without judging them (or yourself). This will lead you to generate powerful ideas and original solutions for your business, your career moves, and your personal life. Let's pause here. Dozens of people within my small social network alone have become crazy rich and/or incredibly fulfilled by combining concepts, blending new technologies with old ideas, or simply applying a Crazytivity approach to their lives. You can do it too by blending the best of who you are today with your new Crazytivity tools.

I truly believe that anyone can learn the mindset I described and the tools you've learned in this book. I regularly teach them in my workshops for companies and entrepreneurs and consistently see amazing results. People just drop a couple of barriers and, in a matter of minutes, you see their imagination flowing again. It is palpable, and it's shockingly impressive!

But it isn't a magic wand. Like any other skill, even if you see exponential results at the beginning, you must be persistent and consistent to master it in the long run. It ISN'T HARD, everyone is capable of it (and it doesn't require more than a few minutes a day), but there is a minimum required if you want to see any change at all.

That is why in my talks, even if I focus on the attitude and the mindset, I also insist on jumping into the action at the end to learn by trial and error. If you do so, it will become easier and easier to look for and find ideas and opportunities around you, to listen to yourself, your intuition, and your little voices—and to have more and more ideas.

So, start something right now. Take an old idea, a phantom project, or simply jump into something that you had in the back of your head. It can be a side project, a new service idea for your business, or a first (among many) brainstorming session on how to unfold your career. It doesn't matter what you start as long as you START now and take your time to complete this project until you've produced something concrete over time. Remember, returning to the exercises and teachings in the book is a great way to refresh your mindset and get inspiration to finish your project. This is the plan for any creative process! See where your explorations lead you, pivot your goals to match your needs as you learn more, tweak, grow, and you'll eventually have a great finished product!

When you are finished or even if you are stuck, write to the Crazytivity community on www.facebook.com/crazytivityclub to tell us about your ideas, projects, doubts, and questions! I'm there to answer them, and your fellow "crazyinnovators" (just invented this word) are here to support you in your creative endeavors.
I believe there is no better way to unleash your creative powers than by trying again and again—and having the support of a community makes celebrating (and bemoaning) the learning curve a lot more fun.

There is a little gift there for you: some lessons are available for free at online-course.butzispeaker.com. One is about our magical moments and how to treat ideas coming to us (a topic explored more in-depth in the book), and the other is an exclusive interview of Ira Seidenstein, a master clown teacher, previously consultant for Cirque du Soleil! Enjoy them!

Anyways, I hope I meet you in person one day so that you can share the results of your creative works with me, whether it is at one of my talks, workshops, or in any other place!

Now, before I let you jump into the unknown with a smile on your face, I want to say thank you. You've read my thoughts (pun intended), and it means a lot to me. You believe in creativity, and that means you now have the power to change the world, even if it is jusr a tiny bit. You are now on a great journey, and I'm really excited for you.

Here is a quote I love that will help you :

"The sea is dangerous and its storms terrible, but these obstacles have never been sufficient reason to remain ashore... unlike the mediocre, intrepid spirits seek victory over those things that seem impossible... it is with an iron will that they embark on the most daring of all endeavors... to meet the shadowy future without fear and conquer the unknown."

- Ferdinand Magellan -

Bon voyage.

Ps: let me know where you landed.

Generate ideas worth millions with Butzi's online course

An in-depth course to unleash immediately your crazy potential!

LEARN
to create new and original ideas

DISCOVER
how to solve your toughest challenges

CREATE
a more meaningful and exciting life by expanding your possibilities

✓ **25** exclusive videos
with powerful practical exercises

✓ An in-depth study of the
Brainstorming Method

✓ **Interviews** with artists and entrepreneurs

✓ My whole creative process
broken down
in step-by-step, digestible lessons
to help you generate amazing ideas!

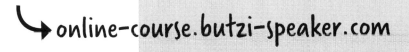

BOOK BUTZI TO SPEAK

Bring magic and Crazytivity to your next event
with an original Keynote Speaker!

BOOST your team's creativity
GENERATE new ideas and solutions everyday
LEARN to create the impossible

Butzi uses his magic as a metaphor and communication tool, sharing stories to bring his audience on a journey they will never forget.
Have Butzi teach you to LIVE the Crazytivity experience and inspire innovation!

More at :

www.butzi-speaker.com

"For the full 45 minutes inspired the 300+ Airbus employees by combining the joy of magic tricks with showing the audience HOW to do it with simple tools and funny stories."

Rey Buckman
AIRBUS

"Very innovative!
A surprising approach that gathers a team around news ways to think differently"

Benedicte Lijour
CAPGEMINI

Acknowledgments

This book would not have existed without the help of my friend and mentor Sonia Choquette, I can't state that enough. She coached me, encouraged me and always gave me honest and constructive feedbacks. Thank you Sonia! If you get a chance, check her work on intuition, it is great and really inspiring!

I also want to thank my wife Diana for her emotional support throughout this process. Her little reminders and encouragements ("Did you write today?", "You should be proud of you...") made all the difference.

For the rest, there is at the same time a million people to thank and the same time no one but the luck I have. I did the writing, I did the thinking, I did everything. It took discipline, patience and a dozen other skills that I didn't have...yet.

But everything I wrote was the product of what I had absorbed in my previous readings and learning experiences. And I'm not even talking about the wonderful education my parents gave me...that is the luck I was talking about: growing up in such an amazing environment. And at the end, it feels like I didn't do anything myself. When I look at this book, it makes me think of a filtered cup of coffee, the coffee and water you usually put in being everything I was taught in my life and the filter being my mind and thoughts.

So, I want to thank my parents and my sister and brother for the education they gave me and made who I am today, but I also want to thank all the entrepreneurs, artists, magicians, teachers, writers and self-development workers who inspired and taught me, directly or throughout their writings.

Here is a list of books that influenced me and that I recommend you to read:

- "Accidental Genius" –Mark Levy–
- "A Whack on the Side of the Head" –Roger Von Oech–
- "The Artist's Way" –Julia Cameron–
- "A day at Elbulli" –Adrià Ferran"
- "Lateral Thinking" –De Bono–
- "What is art?" –Ernst Billgren–

Printed in Poland
by Amazon Fulfillment
Poland Sp. z o.o., Wrocław